NOURISH YOURSELF, NURTURE OUR WORLD

116 plant-focused,
gluten-, grain- and dairy-free recipes
from the Real Coconut Kitchen

DANIELLA HUNTER

Copyright 2020 © by Daniella Hunter

Photographs copyright 2020 © by Anna Fishkin
Cover Image: copyright 2020 © by Oso Parado & Daniella Hunter

Edited by Thea Baumann

All rights reserved.
No part of this publication may be reproduced, stored in a retrieval system, or transmitted, in any form, or by any means, without the prior permission in writing of the publisher or author, nor be otherwise circulated in any form of binding or cover other than that in which it is published and without a similar condition including this condition being imposed on the subsequent purchaser.

The information contained in this book is based on the opinions, ideas and experience of the author. This book is not meant to, nor should it be used, to diagnose or treat any medical condition. For diagnosis or treatment of any medical problem, please consult your own physician. The author and publisher are not responsible for any specific health needs that may require medical supervision and specifically disclaim all responsibility for any liability, loss or risk, personal or otherwise, which is incurred as a consequence, directly or indirectly, of the use and application of any of the contents of this book.

First Edition: May 2020

Book and jacket design by Sarah Hall
igloo-creative.com

The moral right of the author has been asserted.

ISBN 978-1-7349938-0-6

Published by Akasha Publishing (a division of Akasha Global Inc.)
Printed in China

therealcoconut.com
realcoconutkitchen.com

This book is dedicated to all the supporters and fans of the Real Coconut; those who came to eat with us the first day we opened our doors, our regular customers in Tulum and beyond, and the growing community who purchase and enjoy our products. All of you help to nurture and tend to this living, breathing "organism," allowing me and our team to expand our vision further and prove that we can nourish ourselves while nurturing our world.

CONTENTS

INTRODUCTION 9

HOW TO GET STARTED 21

RECIPES

WHERE IT ALL STARTED 41

BREAKFAST 47

SALADS, SOUPS & LIGHT BITES 79

PLATES 119

SWEET TREATS 153

SMOOTHIES, HYDRATION & WARM DRINKS 183

THE BASICS 213

Acknowledgments 243

Index 244

INTRODUCTION

When I first opened the Real Coconut, the tiny beachfront restaurant that operates out of our boutique wellness hotel in Tulum, I could never have imagined how it would grow. What began out of necessity—thinking that we just needed to feed the guests in our 19-room hotel—has, in just five short years, blossomed into a destination restaurant in Tulum (with other locations now opening around the world) and a global food brand—our grain-free coconut flour tortillas and tortilla chips are sold in thousands of stores and online retailers across the USA, Canada and the UK.

I'm not a chef by training and, in some ways, had no business starting a restaurant, but I have to believe that our success is due, at least in part, to exactly that. The food we serve at the Real Coconut is deeply personal. It's the result of my own long and winding journey on the path of health and wellness; the food that makes me feel good, gives me energy, and allows me to operate at optimum level. But it's also much more than that.

The intrinsic philosophy that weaves through all I do, and drives me every day, is a simple question: "How can we care for ourselves at the highest level while also supporting our world?" The Real Coconut has allowed me the opportunity to not only investigate this question at a much larger scale, but also share a small slice of this philosophy with many tens of thousands of people from all walks of life and corners of the planet. This message and food have clearly struck a chord with people, and for that, I am humbled and grateful. So it is finally time to tell the story of how it all came about, provide an in-depth look at why I do what I do, and finally, to share our recipes, something I know many people have been waiting several years for! As with all stories, this one starts at the very beginning . . .

WHERE IT ALL BEGAN

My childhood was defined by my physical weaknesses. Severe asthma led to almost monthly stints in hospital, dealing with chest infections, pneumonia, a collapsed lung, joint dislocations, and other maladies. Playing out my physical deficits on the backdrop of the damp and wet British climate didn't help and yet throughout these challenging experiences, a deep inner strength kept me pushing forward. Though physically weak, I had a feisty nature and endless creative visions. My mother always said that I kept myself busy doing something, even when I could barely breathe!

As I moved into my later teenage years, I experienced some respite from the breathing challenges, and whenever I could, I escaped the dreary UK climate to pursue new experiences and adventures. My love of travel and warm weather led me on a trip to Kenya, where I stumbled upon a tiny scuba-diving center on a remote beach. Despite the fact that lung issues are a major contraindication for diving, my blissful ignorance and deep desire to experience the underwater world led me to self-diagnose my recovery from asthma. Somehow, breathing underwater was the most natural thing in the world for me. I had found myself and my identity through this realm, and this deep love of the sea has gone on to play a pivotal role in the direction of my life.

Soon after graduating from university with a degree in Economics, I set off on a journey of self-discovery to the Red Sea in Sinai, proclaiming to my parents that I was going to pursue a career as a scuba-diving instructor. Dahab, where I based myself, is a remote desert town, with mountains on one side, and some of the world's deepest ocean drop-offs on the other. Somehow this environment—perhaps the sudden boost of vitamin D, along with multiple daily dives—helped heal my lungs and support my body to a point where my new-found strength shocked me. My days as a scuba instructor were blissfully spent on the back of pick-up trucks, driving to shore entry dive sites, walking across rocky reefs with full scuba gear, and swimming against strong currents, often needing to give a helping hand to pull students along with me.

I spent a further stint in the scuba community in Mexico, not far from Tulum, where I turned my hand to underwater photography, but after some years of literally floating around the world, it was time to return to England to pursue a career in photography and writing.

It is important to note that I would never recommend that anyone with lung issues attempt scuba diving without sign-off from their doctor first. My journey began with ignorance and ended well, though the responsibility was always on me. I also believe that the breath-hold freediving, which became part of my daily life, was an additional support in strengthening my lungs.

Back in the UK, my health issues reappeared, and I realized that, without the sun to heal me, I had to take responsibility for my own physical health. I was reminded of a seminar I attended in Dallas as a teenager called "Health Through Nutrition"—where I'd learned all about the effects of diet on our overall well-being—and decided it was time to make some changes.

I had been a very unhealthy vegetarian/vegan for most of my adult life, which meant that my diet was filled with carbohydrates, and without realizing it, a ton of gluten and grains. I can't remember what prompted me to cut out gluten as the first step, but this was when I felt the first shift in my digestion.

For as long as I could remember, I had felt clogged up and constipated, and removing gluten seemed to allow things to move along more smoothly, so to speak.

I began experimenting with gluten-free baking and, having never been able to tolerate dairy well, also embraced a lifestyle of making all that I could at home: nut milks, smoothies, kefirs and more. I would seek out slightly forlorn-looking coconuts on shelves of local Asian markets and crack them open in the garden, often with rain drizzling overhead, imagining myself on a tropical beach. Some of the recipes I created in the UK went on to feature on the menu of the Real Coconut and are still there today!

Though improving my diet helped me somewhat, I was still suffering from a myriad of health issues, and as I had always been drawn to tropical climates, a chance opportunity to stop by Tulum en route to Los Angeles led to a rapid, but carefully considered decision, to pick up and move to Mexico with my husband, Charlie, and my two young sons, Luca and Kai.

Beyond the desire to move back to a tropical climate to support my health, Mexico had always held a special place in my heart. I had such fond memories from my prior time living there, the warmth and openness of the Mexican people and culture, plus Mexican cuisine is my hands-down, all-time favorite! Our first few months were spent acclimatizing to the new lifestyle, and with long balmy days and more free time, I was able to hone my skills in the kitchen further. During this time, I was learning more about gut health, and began to eliminate grains from my diet. This is when I noticed the greatest overall improvement in my well-being. Gluten was one thing, but taking out grains took a huge load off my digestion, and I was finally free of the joint pains and headaches that had plagued me daily, even after our move to Mexico. Confirming my own intuition, I have since been diagnosed with a rare inherited connective tissue disorder, which appears to be aggravated by gluten.

I began experimenting with grain-free baking, using the leftover grounds from my homemade coconut and almond milk. After several successes with coconut flour, in particular, I thought it might work well as a replacement for corn masa—my dear Mayan housekeeper Flor had taught me to make tortillas by hand, and I was determined to figure out how to make a grain-free version. I wanted my recipe to be as close to a traditional tortilla as possible, so including eggs was not an option. But without grains, or anything glutinous to bind them together, my first several attempts were dire failures. I kept at it, though, and through trial and error (of both technique and ingredients), the perfect grain-free coconut flour tortilla was finally born!

Emboldened by my tortilla success, I decided to try my hand at a coconut-based, dairy-free cheese, too. I was never a fan of the go-to cashew-based vegan cheeses, which always made me feel ill, and loved the idea of a dairy-free, grain-free, vegan quesadilla package. It took several failed attempts, but once I found the perfect combination of coconut milk and agar agar (plus a few extras for seasoning), I had the base recipe we still use for all of our vegan cheeses at the restaurant.

My good friends in Tulum would act as taste-testers for me and, to my surprise, raved about all of my whacky grain- and dairy-free experiments! I even hosted a coconut-themed dinner party where I served coconut flour tostadas & guacamole, coconut flour tortillas & coconut cheese for quesadillas, coconut flour pizza topped with coconut "mozzarella," and coconut flour chocolate cake for dessert. It must have gone down well, as they wouldn't stop asking me when the next dinner party would be. I had a feeling I was onto something, but could never have predicted that these fun experiments in my kitchen would soon evolve into a rapidly growing restaurant and food business!

THE BIRTH OF THE REAL COCONUT

Charlie and I had moved to Tulum with a vision to build a boutique wellness hotel—something I'd dreamed of ever since I began my tropical adventures—and six months after we arrived, the opportunity arose to build Sanará. Sanará means "it will heal" in Spanish, and given the healing power of this truly spectacular place, we couldn't think of a more perfect name.

I always imagined myself at the helm of the wellness aspect of the hotel, running the spa and wellness center, and hosting retreats, but the hotel build moved quickly and I soon found myself taking on so much more: reservations for pre-bookings, interior design, and setting up operations included. With so much going on, the restaurant was almost an afterthought—we knew we needed something to serve our guests, but hadn't thought much about the food, and assumed we'd bring in a chef or operator to run it. After all, Tulum had a wonderful culinary scene developing, and we weren't looking to try to compete with that.

But the build continued at a rapid pace and one day, suddenly, our architect team announced that it was time to design the kitchen, and that, in order to plan properly for equipment and layout, we needed the menu. At this point, we hadn't found a chef, didn't have the budget for one, and hadn't the slightest clue about kitchens or restaurants! Perhaps out of necessity, or perhaps from a deeper inner force driving me, I found myself piping up and saying, "give me a couple of weeks and I will come up with one." Looking back, I had no idea where this bold statement would lead me, though I would not have changed it for anything.

I had been watching, with interest, the rise in prevalence of others who were looking to avoid both gluten and grains. Whether due to digestive issues, auto-immune disease, the quest to reduce inflammation, or even just to lose weight, the buzz surrounding gluten- and grain-free eating was exponentially on the rise. Dairy alternatives had also become commonplace in many coffee shops and restaurants, and awareness of the inhumanity and unsustainability of commercial dairy farming was not a new topic. So, during these weeks, as I mulled over the ideas for the restaurant concept, it was clear to me that our menu would not include grain, gluten, or dairy—a concept that I don't believe had been tried before in commercial restaurants, let alone in tiny Tulum!

In my mission to support a movement to promote sustainability, I also had a strong desire to seek out alternatives to the norm, steering away from the go-to crops and foods that dominate our global agricultural economy.

Having seen the most issues around genetic modification and pesticides in corn and soy, in particular, I chose to leave these off our menu. At the same time, I opted to avoid anything that would be the obvious option, or that could cause issues for anyone with a sensitive constitution. This meant no potatoes, no oats, no legumes, no cashews (the go-to dairy-free cheese alternative, but also tough on the digestion), or peanuts. Removing so many of the "usual suspects," which feature in most diets and menus, meant that I had to put a lot of focus on what we were actually able to use. This new approach allowed me to discover and champion what I have come to know as my hero crops: coconut, plantain, cassava, and hemp, for both their nutritional benefits as well as their aspects of sustainability (see Hero

Ingredients on page 30 for further information as to why I love these incredible plants).

As I worked on the menu, I became obsessed about how each recipe would work with different combinations of food choices, and whether it could cause digestive discomfort. This way of menu curating has now become a huge passion of mine. Every dish is designed to complement the others and the overarching concept is that, even if you have eaten well, you still feel light at the end of a meal. You can't really overeat our food (and I personally test all things multiple times, in various combinations, to make sure they don't bother my sensitive tummy).

With the menu complete, and the kitchen build in process, we pulled together a team of local chefs and cooks and began training. Our team would turn up at our apartment with their fizzy soft drinks and look at me strangely as I tried to extoll the benefits of coconuts and grain-free eating in very poor Spanish. I'm sure they thought I was completely mad! And yet, over the years, some of the same team who were with us from the start now use Vitamixes at home, and prepare many of our recipes for their own families. I'm not sure that the Coke and Fanta (or even the corn tortillas) have completely gone, but respect for how food can make you feel and a love of their roles in the overall Real Coconut story is clearly visible.

When we opened our doors at the beginning of 2015, I watched in awe (and slight terror) as people started to trickle into the restaurant. It started with a few of our guests, then people began to wander in from the beach—not even from our hotel—eat, compliment us, and come back again the next day. It was a bizarre experience for me, especially as I had never in my life seen myself as being involved in restaurants.

To this day, I still look around the restaurant when it is buzzing and full, and wonder how on earth this all came to be. People will come up to me and express how grateful they are to have found a spot where they can eat whatever they like, and this kind of appreciation is reflected in our growth as a business. Last New Year, the busiest time in Tulum, in our tiny beach kitchen, where literally everything is made by hand—from cracking open coconuts to make coconut milk, to hand pressing tortillas—we served a record 1,200 customers in one day!

WHERE WE ARE NOW

Charlie and I may have been enjoying a much simpler life, just managing Sanará and the Real Coconut in Tulum, if we had stuck at just that—though anyone who knows us would say that would never have been possible! My love of creating, and Charlie's and my joint passion for asking questions and looking for better ways to do things, along with the pleading requests of guests and customers from around the world, led us to our next stage of evolution, the launch of the Real Coconut products brand. The grain-free tortillas, wraps, and tortilla chips (along with many other products in development) that are now available for purchase in thousands of stores across the US, Canada, UK and beyond, are all born from the initial recipes that I created when I moved to Mexico, and the same recipes that we use in our Tulum restaurant.

Launching and growing a packaged food brand was not something that I had ever intended, but as I reevaluated the purpose behind the birth of the Real Coconut, I homed in on our mission as a company: to offer products that will support many hundreds of thousands of people in their need for alternatives to conventional packaged goods, to support farmers who cultivate sustainable crops using boutique farming methods, and to ultimately work toward delivering this food in sustainable packaging. This mission and purpose is what drives us as we grow the brand.

We now split our time between Tulum and Los Angeles, and while the balance is not always easy, we are blessed to still be able to spend a good amount of time in Tulum, in the pulse of all that is the original Real Coconut. We are currently working on opening our second location in Malibu, with a streamlined, fast-casual menu, and the although the recipes in the book are mostly straight from the menu at our original Tulum location, the food in these pages, and my overall philosophy of eating, are a reflection of our dual lifestyle between the two locations.

Despite the health improvements I have enjoyed along my journey, I still need to respect that my body is extremely delicate, and my position on this path to health is ever-changing. I created the lifestyle I follow to continue to support myself, and as I have shared this through my restaurant and products, I've been blown away by the number of people who it has benefited along the way.

Having started this journey on my own—from my sickly childhood to my days in the kitchen mixing up recipes—the expansion of the vision of the Real Coconut is now supported by a growing team of incredible individuals who walk this path with us and share the same vision and passion. The Real Coconut would not exist without our entire team in Tulum, our incredible chefs in both Tulum and Los Angeles (who have taken my initial concept and recipes and run with them), our products teams in Los Angeles, Minneapolis, and the UK, and of course, my family and close friends who have been by my side, supporting this vision from day one. I could never have foreseen how this would pan out, and could not have done any of this alone. What you read in this book, eat in our restaurants, and buy in our packages, is the culmination of this collective effort, and I am forever grateful to each and every one of our past, current and future team members for the passion and purpose that they bring forward every day that they are with us.

HOW TO GET STARTED

The idea of embarking on a grain-, gluten-, and dairy-free food journey (and leaving behind many of your go-to favorites that you have depended on for your whole life!) may seem daunting at first. Maybe you picked up this book because you have visited the Real Coconut and would love to re-create some of the dishes, or you may have some digestive or health issues and feel that you would like to try to eliminate these groups from your diet. Whatever the reason, please don't feel nervous about starting out. The aim of this book is to provide you not only with delicious, easier to digest versions of some of your favorite dishes, but also a few new techniques and a healthier overall approach to food and cooking!

A chef once said to me, "people go to restaurants to eat food that they can't eat at home," to which I responded, "I want people to come to my restaurant to eat the food that they want to eat at home, or do eat at home!" With this in mind, our menus are always designed to be not only easy to digest but also as honest and simple as possible to make. Any items on our menus that require too many steps or special equipment have been kept out of the book (you'll have to visit one of our restaurants to enjoy them!), and all the recipes here have been reviewed and adjusted for the home cook. This section will give you some starting points to get you prepared before jumping into the recipes.

PLANT-FOCUSED EATING

I often describe our menu as "plant-focused, dairy- and grain-free Mexican-inspired food"—a mouthful, I know! Plant-focused eating means exactly that . . . focus on plants as the basis of your diet, and include carefully considered amounts of high-quality, sustainably sourced animal protein only if and when you feel it's needed. Some people feel they do very well on a fully plant-based diet, and others need the addition of a small amount of animal protein. I can't stress this enough, but the mantra here is "quality over quantity."

Wherever possible, the recipes in this book have options to use a vegan protein alternative, with the exception of only a few dishes. If you do choose to use animal protein, I would recommend pasture-raised, organic chicken, and wild-caught fish or shrimp. I have personally decided to remove even pasture-raised, grass-fed beef from our menus (the only red meat we offered in the past) due to the climate crisis we are facing; however, if you do choose to include this in your diet occasionally, many of our recipes will work with beef as a direct replacement for chicken.

Our favorite plant-based protein alternatives are toasted hemp, sunflower and pumpkin seeds, certain nuts, mushrooms and jackfruit. While jackfruit does not have significant protein content, it makes a wonderful meat replacement texturally—in fact, many people don't even notice they're not eating the "real" thing!

GLUTEN-, GRAIN- & DAIRY-FREE

If you haven't realized it by now, all of our restaurants, menus and recipes are gluten-, grain- and dairy-free! Grain-free inherently means gluten-free, as gluten only exists in certain grains, but we like to reiterate this for anyone who hasn't come across these concepts before.

While we don't use any gluten-containing flours, or grains, there are several grain-free alternatives which feature frequently. I like to keep things simple and stick to our tried and tested favorites, and although I'm sure that new options will be brought forward as more and more people switch to grain-free ways of eating, here are our current choices:

- Coconut Flour
- Cassava Flour
- Cassava Starch (this is the extracted starch from the cassava root, also known as Tapioca)
- Plantain Flour
- Arrowroot Flour/Powder
- Almond Flour
- Ground Pumpkin Seed (works well as a flour replacement in some dishes)
- Chia & Flax Seed (work well as binders where egg is not used)

*If you are avoiding grains and gluten for health reasons, it's important to note that both can be found in some unexpected products. Unless specifically labeled gluten-free, beers and most vodkas contain gluten. Vanilla extract is often alcohol based and unless you are sure of the source of the alcohol, it's best to use either fresh vanilla powder or vanilla bean. In my opinion, these give by far the best flavors, but if you opt to use extract, ensure that it's labeled grain-free.

Certain crops don't fall under the category of the traditional grains, and are often classified as seeds. These are known as pseudo-grains, and common examples are: quinoa, buckwheat, and amaranth, amongst others. If you don't suffer digestive or health issues, it's quite possible that you can happily enjoy these options. I tried for years, but only after identifying our standard go-to grain alternatives, did I finally feel so much better. If you do opt to maintain these in your diet, I would advise traditional preparation methods such as soaking and sprouting.

Removing dairy from the go-to options in the kitchen is less complicated than it seems. Milks made from coconut and almond, coconut yogurt, cheeses, and creams are all things you'll find recipes for in this book, and that we have been serving for over five years in our original restaurant in Tulum. Many people don't even know that we are dairy and grain-free, and they still comment on how much they love the food! Coconut is a great dairy alternative, and I believe it's preferable to almond or other nut milks both in drinks and recipes, as it's a lot more creamy and less allergenic.

ORGANIC VS NON-ORGANIC & WHY QUALITY COUNTS

In our Tulum restaurant, we use organic ingredients wherever possible—something we have been expanding on since we opened in 2015, and which hasn't always been easy in a small beach town. Currently almost all of our produce is grown for us by a couple of local organic providers. Our upcoming restaurants will follow this protocol as well, and it's a philosophy which I also promote for home cooking.

If you have the choice, I always suggest opting for organic produce, particularly for any of the Dirty Dozen fruits and vegetables; those which are known to be grown with the highest amounts of pesticides. These are strawberries, spinach, kale, nectarines, apples, grapes, peaches, cherries, pears, tomatoes, celery, potatoes.[1]

If you are mindful of what you are purchasing, and are careful to avoid wasting produce, or spoilage, then organic doesn't have to be a lot more expensive. To repeat the old adage . . . just remember, quality over quantity.

1. According to the Environmental Working Group, 2019.
www.thepacker.com/article/ewg-releases-2019-dirty-dozen-clean-15-lists

BASE INGREDIENTS

OILS

Our recipes call for only the highest-quality oils, some of which can be heated, and some exclusively for dressings. For cooking, avocado oil and coconut oil are my only choices, with avocado being the preferred choice due to its flavorless profile and high smoke point. For salad dressings or drizzles, extra virgin olive oil or avocado oil are the top options, and for added flavor and nutrient profile, there are a few other cold-pressed oils that work really well: sesame, hemp, pumpkin seed, and flax.

In our restaurants, we exclusively cook with avocado oil, which has the highest smoke point of all edible oils, and therefore can tolerate heating to a high temperature without destabilizing its chemical structure.

SUGAR

In our recipes we try to stick with whole food sweeteners, such as dates, bananas and plantains. As these options don't work in all contexts, my next preferred choices are coconut sugar or coconut nectar, maple syrup, turbinado sugar, muscovado or demerara sugar, more or less in that order! These options are either unrefined or less refined, and still contain certain minerals. We also offer liquid stevia as an addition for drinks at the restaurant. It's important to note, however, that sugar is sugar, whichever way you look at it, so it's more about being mindful on overall consumption of sweet treats.

Monkfruit has become a popular alternative in recent years, though I find the aftertaste slightly bitter. If you don't mind this, feel free to utilize this or your favorite alternative. Other sugar alternatives used heavily in ketogenic and paleo diets are erythritol and xylitol, both sugar alcohols. A number of people complain of digestive discomfort after consuming these, so I have chosen to stay away from them for now.

SALT

We are often conditioned to believe that we should avoid salt, and while I completely agree with avoiding table salt—the refined salt that is used in processed foods and at most restaurants—I personally feel that high-quality, real salt is a beneficial inclusion in our diets. We only use Himalayan pink salt and carefully sourced sea salt in our restaurants, and at home.

NUTS

Although nuts can be ground to make into a flour, we try not to lean too heavily on them as a main flour alternative, opting to use coconut and plantain flour instead wherever possible. This is because, if you think about it, the comparable amount of nuts you would have to eat to get a cup of flour is a huge portion, way more than you would be able to eat in one sitting. The one place where you will find more nuts is in our sweets section, as almond flour helps provide essential texture in egg-free baked goods, but even there, we make an effort to mix in other, more easily digested flours and binders too.

I chose to avoid both cashews and peanuts (which, as you may know, are both technically legumes) from the beginning at the Real Coconut. Peanuts were an obvious choice, being highly allergenic, and the "no cashew" rule arose for two reasons. The first was more personal; I had a really bad experience at a vegan dinner party where cashew was the lead ingredient in every dish. After happily wolfing down all the cheese alternatives, I was ill for days!

As cashew was the go-to option for alternatives to dairy cheese, I opted not to jump on the bandwagon, and by committing to no cashews, our coconut cheese in all its forms has been able to thrive and flourish! I have since met many other people over the years who have had similar experiences with cashews, and are grateful for our no cashew rule!

In addition to the digestive complexities of cashew, there are also concerning questions arising regarding the standards and hand-processing methods used in countries such as India and Vietnam to extract cashews, the shells of which contain harmful cardol and anacardic acid.

LEGUMES
While you won't find legumes on our current menus (with the exception of green peas), I am not against them in all contexts; however, I do find that they can be hard to digest for many people, especially when mixed in with a variety of other dishes and ingredients. I avoid them most of the time, but if you are completely vegan, there may be times when you feel your body needs legumes as a protein source. If you do choose to use them, I would suggest soaking, possibly sprouting, cooking in a pressure cooker, and serving with, for example, some leafy greens and vegetables.

GROUND CHIA/FLAX & EGG REPLACERS
Chia and flax can work wonders as binders and replacements for eggs in many recipes and are best ground in a coffee grinder, Magic Bullet, or NutriBullet.

Some recipes require simply the ground seeds, and others call for a chia or flax gel, which is made by mixing the ground seeds with differing proportions of water.

HERO INGREDIENTS

The following ingredients either form the basis for most of our recipes, or deserve a call-out for their extreme versatility and nutrient content (or both!). All the crops (or organisms, in the case of marine phytoplankton) can provide incredible sustenance to nourish our bodies, while also, when consciously cultivated, supporting farmers in developing countries and creating solutions to feed our burgeoning population.

COCONUT

Our namesake plant, as well as the ingredient that formed the core recipe from where all this began. Coconut palms are, I believe, the most versatile plant in the world, based on all of the products and recipes that can be made from this incredible tree. It's interesting to point out here that coconuts are not by nature of their name a tree nut, despite being classified as such in the US labeling system (no other country in the world classifies coconuts as tree nuts).

While most people think of coconut water as the number one product to come from coconut palms, I am not a fan of mass production or consumption of coconut water from young coconuts. When a coconut is bright green and still hanging from the tree, the only thing that can be obtained is the water; yet by waiting a couple of months, the coconut will mature and a magical process takes place inside, where some of the water is absorbed to form a layer of "meat." By the time the coconut has fallen to the ground, it can provide multiple products: water (yes, there is still some water inside, and it tastes great); coconut oil and coconut cream (from expeller-pressing the flesh); and the dry residue becomes coconut flour. From these four basic ingredients, a literal smorgasbord of recipes can be made! While producing the whole coconuts, certain fronds of the tree can be simultaneously "tapped" to obtain coconut nectar, coconut vinegar, and even coconut aminos, reminiscent of tamari or soy sauce. This bountiful plant is known as the Tree of Life in Asia, and I couldn't agree more!

As well as being versatile, coconuts are considered by many cultures as a true superfood, both for the multitude of vitamins, minerals and beneficial fat content of coconut cream, milk and oil and the high fiber found in coconut flour.

PLANTAIN

Soon after we opened the restaurant, I had an "aha" moment while traveling down to Belize to visit some coconut farmers. As we drove through this tiny country, I saw plantain trees everywhere! When I questioned the farmers, they explained that they grow like weeds; even if you barely tend to them, they still grow and mature in only ten months! I wondered why they weren't used more as a food source, apart from as a side to rice and beans, either baked or fried. We were already making our pancakes and some cakes using fresh plantains, but I pondered how we could use this easy to digest, and abundant, plant in more dishes.

In addition to being a sustainable crop, plantain is also high in resistant starch (a recent buzz-term in the digestive health world), which acts as a gut microbe–feeding prebiotic, so it checks even more boxes!

Back in Mexico, I sourced plantain flour (often known as green banana flour), and began testing this in a bread, as well as other baked goods. I made it my mission to introduce plantain as a potential major food source to the world, and now so many of our recipes, and those in this book, feature both fresh plantain and plantain flour.

My hope is to see this bountiful ingredient as a commonplace staple on supermarket shelves, and by extension, support the farmers who can benefit from a new economy on a plant that is almost organic by nature, based on how easily it grows. In fact, I love this plant and use it so much that I could almost have called the brand the "Real Plantain," but doubt that would have had so much appeal!

CASSAVA

Along with coconut and plantain, cassava (also known as yucca) is another plant that features frequently in our recipes and on our menu. Also high in beneficial resistant starch, cassava tubers grow in similar conditions to plantains and coconuts, is equally easy to cultivate, and matures within ten months. Cassava flour is a staple in the Real Coconut kitchen, both whole and in its form as extracted starch, commonly known as tapioca. Yucca fries are our alternative to french fries, and the fresh root can be cooked and mashed to form the basis of a number of other recipes. Another reason that cassava sits in my top three hero crops is that it has recently been used to make a biodegradable replacement for plastic bags, which animals and marine life can actually eat!

HEMP

Our go-to plant-based protein, I could sing the praises of hemp in its own chapter, but for brevity, I'll simply say that this plant is a powerhouse. The seeds are able to provide a high-nutrient, plant-based protein content, while the rest of the plant offers sustainable solutions for so many of our day-to-day needs, from construction to plastic alternatives and paper; it even helps clean and replenish our soil!

MARINE PHYTOPLANKTON

Although not an easy ingredient to include in recipes, but something that I consume daily, my top whole-food, nutritional superhero must be called out to make this book complete. In fact, marine phytoplankton is so important that, depending on the season, it provides 50-80% of the oxygen in our atmosphere and oceans. With rising ocean temperatures and pollution, phytoplankton numbers are declining, and in some areas, the fish are literally suffocating from lack of oxygen in the water. I source our phytoplankton from a pure water source in the Netherlands and use it as my alternative to supplements. It provides a highly bio-available source of vitamins and nutrients, and is the only known form of EPA (an essential fatty acid that usually needs to be converted, at a high energy cost, from ALA in vegan food sources). I actually have a gut feeling that marine phytoplankton will be so important in the future, it may be one of our primary sources of nutrition.

STOCKING UP: DRY INGREDIENTS

We use a few lesser-known dry ingredients that, while sometimes difficult to source at your local grocery store, can be found in some natural food stores, or easily ordered online:

COCONUT FLOUR — Believe it or not, the type of coconut flour does make a difference in tortilla making – I prefer a slightly toasted, very fine coconut flour like Bob's Red Mill.

PLANTAIN FLOUR — Also known as green banana flour—green plantains are simply dried and ground into a flour.

CASSAVA FLOUR — This is the whole cassava flour, not the starch.

TAPIOCA FLOUR — Also known as tapioca starch or cassava starch—the extracted starch from the cassava root.

ARROWROOT STARCH — Another starch alternative.

PSYLLIUM HUSK POWDER/FLAKES — A dietary fiber made from the husks of the Plantago plant's seeds and used as a binder in several of our recipes.

AGAR AGAR POWDER — A natural seaweed-based gelatin alternative. We use a UK brand called Jalpurs, which is available on Amazon, or Living Jin. The only brand we have found that doesn't work so well is Now Foods.

XANTHAN GUM — Optional for use in homemade tortillas, xanthan gum is a polysaccharide created through a process of fermentation and is a common addition in gluten-free recipes.

PROBIOTIC CAPSULES — We like Jarrow Formulas.

DEHYDRATED JACKFRUIT — We use this as a substitute for animal protein. The whole fruit is literally enormous, so this is an easy way to have jackfruit available whenever you need it.

COCONUT AMINOS — A soy-free alternative to soy sauce.

LIQUID SMOKE — To provide a hint of barbecue flavor.

COCONUT MILK — Canned, preferably free from gums and BPA.

STOCKING UP: FRESH PRODUCE

Most of the fresh produce referred to in our recipes is easy to find in most supermarkets or farmers markets. Fresh, mature coconuts are now readily available; however, we always offer options to use already prepared coconut milk.

Cassava, or yucca, is a root vegetable and can be found in most supermarkets, either fresh or peeled and frozen.

Fresh plantains are used frequently in our recipes and, as they are not so well used or known in traditional Western cooking, they deserve more of an explanation. Plantains are a larger and more starchy cousin of the banana. They can be increasingly found in many major supermarkets and natural foods or specialty markets, but not always at the right stage of ripeness! If in doubt, choose green plantains, as you can ripen them at home, although they can take longer to ripen than bananas.

- Green plantains are very starchy and not sweet. At this stage, their skins are tough, making them difficult to open. To peel, you can either blanch them for a minute in boiling water or cut into chunks and slice off the skin. You can also freeze grated green plantains for future use.
- Medium-ripe plantains are yellow with some black spots and are slightly sweet. By this point, the skin is easy to peel.
- Ripe plantains have black skins, are soft to the touch and are sweet. These need to be used quickly and work well for cakes and, to some extent, pancakes. (Medium-ripe and ripe plantains can also be frozen for later use.)

TIP: Ripen plantains in a brown paper bag, preferably with other produce such as bananas or apples.

EQUIPMENT

The recipes in this book can be made with equipment that most home cooks will have in their kitchen. Some useful pieces of equipment that we regularly use and can be purchased online are:

- High-Powered Blender, such as a Vitamix
- Nutribullet/Magic Bullet or Coffee Grinder
- Stand Mixer
- Cook's Thermometer
- Nut Milk Bag
- Tortilla Press
- Coconut Tool™ (Essential for Extracting Meat from Coconuts!)

PREPARING IN BULK

To make life easier, many of our recipes can be made in multiple batches to freeze, or to keep on hand in the pantry or fridge, without making extra work. The same bases are also used in many recipes (for example, the coconut cheese and yogurt), so it's worth doubling or even tripling in these cases, making it easy to put together more dishes through the week.

I recommend storing batches of recipes in either tempered glass dishes (designed for freezing), or reusable silicone storage bags.

HOW TO OPEN A COCONUT

I'm not going to lie; opening coconuts and prying out the meat is not the easiest of tasks, and I have huge respect for our team in Tulum who do this with a ridiculous number of coconuts every day! When I used to do this back in England, it was a kind of therapy for me—I imagined myself living on a tropical island and foraging on the land, and it became a bit of a meditation. If you're looking for your own coconut meditation, here's how to do it:

- Try to select the freshest coconuts. Pick them up and give them a good shake–they will be the ones most filled with the water. You can also request coconuts at your local health-foods store, or Whole Foods Market.
- Use a hammer to open. Hold the coconut in your hand and using the hammer, hit once on the circumference, then turn it slightly, hit again, turn, hit, turn, hit. Repeat this process (it can take a while if the coconut is tougher and has been sitting around for a long time) until you hear a change in the sound. Get ready with a bowl or pitcher underneath, and keep hitting and turning. Finally, you should hear a crack and the water will start to run out. Let it drain over the bowl, and then keep hitting and turning until it's fully opened (for a video, visit our restaurant Instagram account, @realcoconutkitchen).
- Using a short pointed knife or a Coconut Tool (may be purchased on Amazon), pry into the edge of where the meat joins the shell, taking care not to slip. If you are lucky, you may be able to pry out the entire half of the meat in one or two tries. If it's really not happening, use the hammer to break up the shell into further pieces (this is where you can really lay into it!) and use the knife or tool to pry out the meat from the smaller pieces.
- Once you have the meat from the shell, break it into small pieces and follow the steps on page 215 to make the milk.
- This meat can also be used for coconut bacon (remove the brown skin and use a vegetable peeler to make strips—see page 225).

RECIPES

Symbols Key:

 Vegan/Vegan Option

 Contains Eggs

 Contains Nuts

 Freezable

 Skill: Easy, Medium or Hard

IN THE BEGINNING . . .

This book (and the entire menu at the Real Coconut!) simply would not exist without my coconut flour tortillas and chips, so I decided they deserve their own section. In Tulum, our incredible team makes these by hand every day, with love and care, but you certainly don't need a professional kitchen to do so. If you've made masa tortillas by hand before, you'll find that our coconut flour version requires a few more steps, but employs a very similar technique; if you haven't, don't be intimidated! We've broken the process down into a clear, step-by-step guide that even the most inexperienced cooks will be able to follow. It may take you a couple of tries to master, but once you get the hang of the recipe (and have a feel for the tortilla press), you'll be making these with your eyes closed! There is nothing quite like a fresh tortilla, still hot from the pan, or a just-fried chip, lightly showered in Himalayan pink salt, but if you're short on time (or just don't feel up to making these from scratch), both our tortillas and chips are readily available in stores and online.

COCONUT FLOUR TORTILLAS

MAKES 14 - 16 TORTILLAS

You just can't beat the texture and flavor of freshly made tortillas; plus the satisfaction of cooking something like this from scratch is unparalleled. If you don't have time to make them by hand, you can always buy our packaged tortillas, but I urge you to give these a whirl—even once for a special occasion or to impress your friends! The dough is simple to make, and once you get the hang of pressing the tortillas, you'll be surprised how easy it can be. You can also half-cook these and freeze to have available whenever you need them. So grab some coconut flour and a tortilla press (these can be easily sourced on Amazon), invite some friends over, and start mixing!

INGREDIENTS:

⅔ cup / 80g coconut flour

½ cup / 60g tapioca flour

½ teaspoon / 3g Himalayan pink salt

½ teaspoon / 3g xanthan gum or

3 teaspoons / 12g ground chia

approx 6 ounces / 160g water

avocado oil

METHOD:

1) Stir together coconut flour, tapioca, salt and xanthan or ground chia, making sure that the dry ingredients are thoroughly distributed.

2) Add the water, a little at a time, slowly stirring in. The mixture will start dry, and gradually thicken with the water to form a dough. Keep adding more water, kneading in between. Be careful not to add too much water, as it's hard to go back!

3) Using your hands, knead the mixture until a dough forms (a few minutes). Let the dough sit for 5 minutes, as coconut flour tends to absorb more water after a little time. The dough should be soft and malleable. If it feels dry, you can add a tablespoon of water at a time, and knead to get the correct consistency.

4) For 5-inch tortillas, divide the dough into around 15 equal portions (they should each weigh about 20g). Place each ball between 2 small squares of parchment paper and gently flatten in a tortilla press. Turn, and press again if the tortilla feels too thick.

5) Heat a nonstick sauté pan and add a spray of avocado oil. Very carefully, peel the parchment away and cook the tortillas for about 1-2 minutes per side, until lightly browned.

6) Use immediately or hold cooked tortillas in a damp cloth until ready to use.

7) To reheat, warm the tortillas on both sides, in a lightly greased pan.

COCONUT FLOUR TORTILLA CHIPS

SERVES 2 - 4

Like the tortillas, fresh, homemade tortilla chips can't be beaten for their flavor. The tortillas form the base of these chips, and you will go through a lot of them to make these, so preparing the tortillas in advance is a must (if you can source our packaged tortillas, you can also use those). Frying definitely gives the best flavor, but I also enjoy the baked version. If you fry or bake a whole tortilla, you'll get a tostada, which is used for several of our recipes.

INGREDIENTS:

1 recipe Coconut Flour Tortillas (p. 43) or store-bought

avocado oil

OPTION 1: FRY

1) In a deep skillet, heat 1-1½ inches of avocado oil to 350°F.
2) Cut each tortilla into 8 wedges. Carefully drop the wedges into the oil one handful at a time, making sure they don't stick together. Fry until golden brown on both sides, turning as necessary.
3) Drain on a wire rack or over paper towels.

OPTION 2: OVEN BAKE

1) Preheat oven to 350°F.
2) Cut each tortilla into 8 wedges. Brush each wedge with a little bit of avocado oil and arrange on a sheet pan, making sure to leave space between each one.
3) Bake for 15-20 minutes, until crispy.

BREAKFAST

Breakfast is my absolute favorite meal but ironically, I don't actually like eating it in the morning. I'm known in Tulum for ordering my favorites (like Eggs Benedict or Hash Browns) when everyone else is eating lunch, and even sometimes in the evenings! Some might call this pattern of eating intermittent fasting—where you consume all of your meals within an 8-hour window and fast for the remaining 16, allowing the body a longer period of rest from digestion. I don't label it as such, and don't adhere to any strict rules or schedules when it comes to my meals, but I've been naturally eating this way for decades, and it seems to work well for my body.

Whether you're a "breakfast upon rising" type of person or in the "eggs for dinner" camp (or both!), you're sure to find something in this chapter to satisfy your cravings. The lighter dishes like yogurts or cereals can work especially well as an evening option if you've had a big lunch, and don't miss out on the Macho Pancakes (page 56) or Buttermilk Pancakes (page 58) for the ultimate lazy weekend treat!

COCONUT YOGURT

SERVES 4

Coconut yogurt is a staple in our kitchens, both at home and at the restaurant, as it forms the base of several breakfast dishes, and many of our sauces and dressings. You may think that making yogurt from scratch is complicated; it's really not! Once you get used to making it, you'll be able to whip this up in no time flat. I've included the recipe for Super Sprinkles here, as they pair so well with this yogurt. Keep the rest in an airtight container for several weeks. I'm also partial to a generous drizzle of raspberry coulis, but you really can make this your own by adding any combination of mix-ins you like. This will last at least a week in the fridge, so it's definitely worth doubling or even tripling the recipe.

FOR THE YOGURT:

6 tablespoons / 50g tapioca flour

4¼ cups / 1000g Coconut Milk (p. 215) or canned

4 teaspoons / 15g maple syrup

4 capsules probiotic

FOR THE SUPER SPRINKLES MIX:

1/4 cup / 12g toasted coconut flakes

1 tablespoon / 10g chia seed

1 tablespoon / 9g Toasted Hemp (p. 222)

1 tablespoon / 9g cacao nibs

2 tablespoons / 15g almonds, roughly chopped

METHOD:

1) Pour boiling water into a container to sterilize. Discard the water and allow to air dry.

2) In a medium saucepan, whisk to combine the tapioca flour, coconut milk and maple syrup. Heat over a low flame, stirring constantly, until thickened and small bubbles form (about 15 minutes).

3) Transfer to the sterilized container and allow the mixture to cool to below 107°F.

4) Open the probiotic capsules and pour the contents into the yogurt mixture; whisk well. It's important that the mixture is tepid, not hot; if too hot, the probiotics will be damaged and the yogurt will not ferment properly.

5) Cover and store at room temperature for 24-36 hours to ferment. When it's ready, the yogurt will have a tangy flavor and be slightly thickened.

6) Transfer to the refrigerator and chill before serving.

7) Serve with berries, a tablespoon of Super Sprinkles and Raspberry Coulis (p. 238).

TIP: The yogurt will take shorter or longer to ferment depending on the ambient temperature. In cooler climates, try to find a warm spot (up on a shelf or next to a warm oven, for example) to keep the mixture. In warmer climates, check the mixture earlier and more often, as the fermenting process may happen more quickly.

& CINNAMON CEREAL

wanted a grain-free cereal that was not all nuts, and developed the original version of this recipe back in England before we even moved to Mexico! It's so simple to throw together, makes a great work or travel snack, and keeps in an airtight container for at least a month. I love the crunch from the plantain pieces, but if you're short on time, the base mix is still delicious on its own.

FOR THE DRIED PLANTAIN MIX:

2 green plantains
¼ cup / 78g maple syrup
¼ cup / 78g coconut oil, melted
Pinch Himalayan pink salt

FOR THE BASE MIX:

1 cup / 172g chia seeds
1 cup / 160g Toasted Hemp (p. 222)
1½ cups / 247g raisins
1½ cups / 247g dried apple, chopped
1 cup / 145g almonds, chopped
2 teaspoons / 6g ground cinnamon

TO MAKE THE DRIED PLANTAINS:

1) Preheat the oven to 250°F.
2) Peel and slice the plantains into very thin discs.
3) Toss with maple syrup, coconut oil and salt. Spread out in a single layer on a baking sheet lined with parchment paper or a silicone mat. Bake for about 50 minutes.
4) Turn the oven off, but leave the plantains inside for about 4-5 hours to dehydrate completely. They should be very crispy.
5) Allow to cool completely.

TO MAKE THE CEREAL:

1) Mix together the dried plantains, chia seeds, toasted hemp, raisins, dried apple, almonds and cinnamon.

TO SERVE:

1) Serve with your favorite plant-based milk or yogurt, sliced bananas and berries. For a crunchier cereal, eat immediately, or let the milk soak in for around 10 minutes in the fridge before enjoying.

CHOCOLATE CEREAL

SERVES 10   **M**

A chocolatey spin on the Apple & Cinnamon Chia Cereal. I always have a big batch (I make a bulk amount of 2 - 3 times this recipe!) in my pantry on hand for an easy breakfast or snack.

FOR THE DRIED PLANTAIN MIX:

2 green plantains

¼ cup / 78g maple syrup

¼ cup / 78g coconut oil, melted

Pinch Himalayan pink salt

FOR THE BASE MIX:

1 cup/ 172g chia seeds

1 cup / 160g Toasted Hemp (p. 222)

1 cup / 175g Medjool dates, pitted and chopped small

1 cup / 145g almonds, roughly chopped

2 tablespoons / 15g cacao powder

1 cup / 120g cacao nibs

TO MAKE THE DRIED PLANTAINS:

1) Preheat the oven to 250°F.
2) Peel and slice the plantains into very thin discs.
3) Toss with maple syrup, coconut oil and salt. Spread out in a single layer on a baking sheet lined with parchment paper or a silicone mat. Bake for about 50 minutes.
4) Turn the oven off, but leave the plantains inside for about 4-5 hours to dehydrate completely. They should be very crispy.
5) Allow to cool completely.

TO MAKE THE CEREAL:

1) Mix together the dried plantain, chia seeds, toasted hemp, dates, almonds and cacao nibs.
2) Sift the cacao powder over the mixture and toss to coat. You can store the cereal mix at room temperature in an airtight container for about a month.

TO SERVE:

1) Serve with your favorite plant-based milk or yogurt. I prefer coconut or almond. Eat right away if you prefer a crunchier cereal; otherwise, chill for 10 minutes in the fridge to allow the chia to soften.

BLENDED CHOCOLATE CHIA PUDDING

MAKES 4 (1/2 CUP) SERVINGS

I literally made this recipe every day for about a year when we were building Sanará. It's so easy, healthy and delicious; I don't think I could ever get tired of it! Try popping this in the freezer until it's partially frozen—it feels and tastes like eating ice cream for breakfast.

INGREDIENTS:

2 cups / 480g Coconut Milk (p. 215) or canned
5 Medjool dates, pitted
3 tablespoons / 22g cacao powder
½ teaspoon / 2g vanilla extract
¼ cup / 80g maple syrup
¼ cup / 43g chia seeds
berries for garnish

METHOD:

1) Combine the milk, dates, cacao powder, vanilla extract and maple syrup in a blender; blend until smooth. Add the chia and continue to blend, scraping any chia seeds down from the sides as needed.
2) Spoon into small bowls or mason jars. Cover and refrigerate for at least a couple of hours and up to 4 days.
3) Serve with mixed berries.

SEASONAL CHIA PARFAIT

SERVES 4

Although this seems like a bit of work to put together, if your chia jam and coconut yogurt are already made, it's actually an easy (and very impressive!) make-ahead breakfast option. I love to mix this up, using whatever fruits are in season for the jam and topping—apples or pears in the winter, stone fruit or berries in the summer. If you're making this for a crowd, or just don't feel like fussing with individual jars, feel free to assemble this in one large bowl instead.

INGREDIENTS:

4 tablespoons / 56g chia seeds

¼ teaspoon / 1g vanilla extract or

½ teaspoon / 2.5g vanilla powder

1 cup / 240g Coconut Milk (p. 215) or canned

1 cup / 325g Blueberry Chia Jam (p. 62)

1 cup / 235g Coconut Yogurt (p. 49) or store-bought

mixed berries

mint sprigs

METHOD:

1) In a bowl, whisk together the chia seeds, vanilla and coconut milk until combined; refrigerate for a couple of hours.

2) Follow with a layer of jam and a layer of yogurt in equal proportions to fill the jar.

3) Top with berries and mint just before serving.

TIP: The batter will keep in the fridge for 2 days. Cooked pancakes can also be frozen, then reheated in a skillet, oven or toaster. If you do plan to make a big batch and freeze, we suggest undercooking them slightly so they won't dry out too much when reheated.

MACHO PANCAKES

SERVES 2

People always ask me why this recipe is called Macho Pancakes, and the answer is simple! In Spanish, plantain is called "platano macho," so I think I just started calling it this at home and the name stuck. This is by far one of the most popular breakfasts in Tulum! We serve these with bananas, berries, raspberry coulis and maple syrup at the restaurant, but they also make a brilliant savory plate topped with avocados and cherry tomatoes. This makes excellent waffles, too!

Once you get the hang of the recipe you can do it with your eyes closed, but there are a number of caveats to keep in mind, depending on what plantains you can find, and even what to do if you can't find them!

Medium-ripe plantains are yellow with some black spots. Very ripe plantains, or even normal bananas will work, but may require additional plantain flour to thicken the recipe. If you can only find green plantains, you can divide the amount into plantains and ripe bananas, to get the same effect. For a more savory pancake, green plantains work and you won't need the flour.

INGREDIENTS:

2 large / 375g medium-ripe plantains

⅓ vanilla bean (or ½ teaspoon / 2g vanilla extract or ¼ teaspoon / 1g vanilla powder)

3 large eggs (or 4 medium eggs)

1 teaspoon / 3g baking soda

¼ cup / 35g coconut oil

¼ - ⅓ cup / 35 - 45g plantain flour

METHOD:

1) Break the plantains into chunks and place in a high-powered blender with the vanilla bean, eggs, baking soda and coconut oil. Blend for approximately 1 minute, until smooth. Add the plantain flour and blend until completely incorporated.

2) If you have time, let the batter sit in the fridge for 20 minutes or longer (batter can be made ahead and kept for up to 2 days in an airtight container in the refrigerator).

3) Heat a nonstick pan over medium flame, pour in about ¼ cup of the batter, and cook until small bubbles form in the center. Flip and continue cooking until browned. Continue with the remaining batter. If making waffles, cook the batter, ¼ cup at a time, in a lightly greased waffle iron until golden brown.

BUTTERMILK PANCAKES

MAKES 8 PANCAKES   E

So fluffy and moist, people never believe these incredible pancakes are vegan! The buttermilk gives a great flavor here, but if you're in a rush, they can be made with a dairy-free milk of your choice instead.

FOR THE COCONUT BUTTERMILK:

1 cup / 240g Coconut Milk (p. 215) or canned

1 tablespoon / 14g lemon juice

1 tablespoon / 14g apple cider vinegar

FOR THE PANCAKE MIX:

¼ cup plus 2 teaspoons / 60g coconut oil, melted

½ cup / 100g coconut buttermilk

¼ cup / 68g unsweetened applesauce

1½ teaspoons / 8g apple cider vinegar

⅓ cup / 40g coconut sugar

½ cup plus 5 teaspoons / 58g almond flour

½ cup / 58g tapioca

½ cup / 58g coconut flour

1¾ teaspoon / 8g baking soda

1½ teaspoons / 8g baking powder

pinch Himalayan pink salt

avocado oil, for coating pan

berries and maple syrup, to serve

TO MAKE THE BUTTERMILK:

1) Stir together the coconut milk, lemon juice and apple cider vinegar.
2) Cover and place in the refrigerator overnight.

TO MAKE THE PANCAKES:

1) Whisk together the coconut oil, buttermilk, applesauce, apple cider vinegar and coconut sugar. Add the dry ingredients and whisk well to combine.
2) Heat the avocado oil in a nonstick sauté pan over low heat.
3) Spoon ¼ cup of the batter into the pan and spread out into a 4-inch circle (the batter will be thick). Cook over low heat until bubbles appear in the middle and the edges start to look dry. Flip and cook for another 3-4 minutes, until browned.
4) Serve with fresh berries and maple syrup.

PLANTAIN FLOUR BREAD

MAKES ONE 9" LOAF

This is one of our signature recipes and revolutionary in the world of grain-free baking! Plantain flour is easy on the digestion, making this the only bread we serve at our restaurants. This recipe can come out slightly denser when made in lower levels of humidity, but works really well toasted and loaded with spreads, or as an open sandwich. For English muffins, simply bake the dough in a muffin top baking pan instead.

INGREDIENTS:

- 3½ ounces / 50g water
- 2 tablespoons / 20g ground chia seeds
- 8 ounces / 250g water
- ½ cup / 100g extra virgin olive oil
- 2 teaspoons / 6g apple cider vinegar
- 3⅓ cups / 400g plantain flour
- ¾ teaspoon / 4g Himalayan pink salt
- ½ teaspoon / 8g baking soda
- 4½ ounces / 125ml warm water
- 1½ tablespoons / 30g maple syrup
- 1 (¼ ounce) / 7g package active dry yeast

METHOD:

1) In a small bowl, stir together the 3½ ounces of water and the ground chia seeds to make "chia gel." Set aside.
2) In the bowl of a stand mixer, combine the 8 ounces of water, extra virgin olive oil, apple cider vinegar, plantain flour, salt and baking soda. Mix on low using the beater attachment.
3) In another small bowl, stir together the 4½ ounces of warm water, maple syrup and active dry yeast until yeast is dissolved.
4) Cover with a towel and place in a warm spot for 5 minutes to allow the yeast to activate; the mixture will be fluffy and foamy.
5) Add the chia gel to the dough in the stand mixer; beat on low/medium speed to combine. Add the yeast mixture and beat on low/medium speed until well incorporated.
6) Grease a loaf pan and line it with parchment paper; grease again.
7) Transfer the dough to the prepared pan and smooth out the top with a spatula. If making English muffins, divide the dough into a greased muffin top baking pan instead. Cover with a damp towel and leave in a warm spot for 45 minutes to rise.
8) Meanwhile, preheat the oven to 350°F.
9) Uncover the bread and bake for 45-50 minutes (if making English muffins, bake for 15-20 minutes). Bread is done when a skewer inserted into the center comes out clean.
10) Store in an airtight container at room temperature for up to 3 days, in the refrigerator for up to 2 weeks, or in the freezer for several months.

TIP: If you don't have a stand mixer, this bread still works well but will need some elbow grease to beat the dough.

TOAST & SPREADS

SERVES 1 **E**

One of the top breakfast choices at the Real Coconut is our "Toast and Spreads" offering, which is all about customization. Each serving has a few slices of our famous plantain bread (toasted, of course), and little pots of chocolate hazelnut spread, chia jam, honey, and almond butter, plus sliced banana. Guests can mix and match, adding as much or as little of each as they want, to make their own perfect combo! My favorite is almond butter, honey & bananas. I can't get enough of it!

INGREDIENTS:

3 slices plantain bread, toasted
2 tablespoons / 36g chocolate hazelnut spread
2 tablespoons / 40g Blueberry Chia Jam
2 tablespoons / 48g Almond Butter (p. 223) or store-bought
2 tablespoons / 30g honey
1 small / 105g banana, sliced

TO SERVE:

1) Place the hazelnut spread, chia jam, almond butter, and honey in small serving bowls.
2) Serve the toasted bread with all of the spreads and the sliced banana on the side.

CHOCOLATE HAZELNUT SPREAD

⅓ cup / 160g maple syrup
½ cup / 60g cacao powder
⅓ cup / 6 g coconut oil
2¼ cups / 300g hazelnuts
pinch / 1g Himalayan pink salt
1¼ cups / 300g Almond Milk (p. 216) or store-bought

1) Blend all ingredients in a food processor until completely smooth.
2) Use immediately or store in an airtight container in the fridge for up to 2 weeks.

BLUEBERRY CHIA JAM

1½ cups / 200g frozen blueberries
1 cup / 250ml water
2 teaspoons / 8g chia seeds
2 tablespoons / 25g maple syrup

1) Combine all ingredients in a saucepan and cook over medium flame for 20 minutes, stirring occasionally. Remove from the heat and let cool to room temperature.
2) Use immediately or store in an airtight container in the fridge for up to 2 weeks.

AVOCADO TOAST

SERVES 1

The ubiquitous avocado toast is a staple on most menus, but finding a grain-free version is almost impossible. Using our original plantain bread recipe, this could be the best avocado toast on the planet!

INGREDIENTS:

2 slices Plantain Bread (p. 60)

1 medium / 136g avocado, cubed

1 tablespoon / 14g lime juice

½ teaspoon / 4g Himalayan pink salt

pinch black pepper

1 tablespoon / 3g sunflower sprouts or microgreens

pinch chili flakes, optional

METHOD:

1) Toast the bread slices well.

2) In a small bowl, gently toss together the avocado, lime juice, salt and pepper; spoon onto the toast.

3) Top with sunflower sprouts and chili flakes for a slightly spicy kick.

BAGELS

MAKES 5 BAGELS   M

I know making bagels from scratch may seem daunting, but once you've got the hang of it, they're actually really easy (promise!). Because they do take a bit of time, I always cook a big batch and store any extras in the freezer—just don't forget to toast before serving. These are delicious with dairy-free cream cheese, smoked salmon and cucumber, but my favorite way to enjoy them is with a fried egg, avocado, spinach and mustard. It's very messy, but worth it!

INGREDIENTS:

1 (¼ oz.) package active dry yeast
2 tablespoons / 25g maple syrup
7 oz. / 200g warm water (about 105°F-110°F)
⅓ cup / 75g cassava flour
½ cup / 55g arrowroot
⅓ cup + 2 teaspoons / 50g coconut flour
½ cup / 50g toasted pumpkin seed, ground
⅓ cup / 40g ground flax
¾ teaspoon / 6g Himalayan pink salt
1 tablespoon / 15g apple cider vinegar
avocado oil for brushing

METHOD:

1) In a small bowl, stir together the yeast, maple syrup and warm water. Cover with a towel and place in a warm spot until the yeast mixture is foamy and fluffy (about 5 minutes).
2) In a medium bowl, stir together the dry ingredients. Add yeast mixture and stir until well incorporated.
3) Knead dough for about 5 minutes; the dough will be slightly sticky, so dust your hands with a bit of cassava flour if needed. Separate the dough into 5 equal balls.
4) Bring a medium pot (about 3 quarts) of water to a boil and add the apple cider vinegar.
5) Flatten the dough balls slightly and poke a hole in the center of each with your finger, making a ring. Carefully place each dough ring, one at a time, into the boiling water and cook for 1 minute per side.
6) Remove the bagels from the boiling water and place on a sheet pan lined with parchment paper. Brush the tops with a small amount of avocado oil and bake for 1 hour 30 minutes.
7) Remove from the oven and allow to cool COMPLETELY before slicing in half.
8) Store at room temperature in an airtight container for 2 days, in the refrigerator for up to 1 week, or in the freezer for several months.

SWEET POTATO & PLANTAIN HASH BROWN

MAKES 6 PATTIES   M

Our Real Coconut take on the traditional hash brown uses a mixture of plantain and sweet potato for a lighter flavor. The tangy green tomatillo sauce is the perfect accompaniment and keeps in the refrigerator for up to four days. We normally serve these with a lightly dressed salad and avocado, but if you're looking for a heartier meal, try topping the patties with poached or scrambled eggs.

FOR THE PATTIES:

2 large/ 300g sweet potatoes, peeled and grated

2 small / 200g green plantains, peeled and grated

2 teaspoons / 10g avocado oil + additional for frying

2 tablespoons / 25g yellow onion, finely diced

1 teaspoon / 25g ground chia seeds

8 tablespoons / 125g water

1 teaspoon / 5g Chipotle Chile Paste (p. 235)

1 teaspoon / 8g Himalayan pink salt

½ teaspoon / 2g black pepper

FOR THE SAUCE:

1 bulb garlic

6 medium / 250g tomatillos

1 teaspoon Himalayan pink salt

½ teaspoon black pepper

TO SERVE:

1 cup mixed baby greens

1 tablespoon extra virgin olive oil

1 teaspoon lemon juice

pinch Himalayan pink salt

pinch black pepper

1 avocado, diced

TO MAKE THE SAUCE:

1) Preheat oven to 350°F.
2) Wrap the garlic bulb in foil and roast in the oven for 1 hour 20 minutes. Remove and allow to cool.
3) Peel the papery skin from the outside of the tomatillos and lightly rub each one under running water to remove any dirt.
4) Squeeze the roasted garlic bulbs out of their skins and into a blender. Add the tomatillos, salt and pepper; blend until smooth.

TO MAKE THE PATTIES:

1) Preheat the oven to 350°F.
2) Spread the grated sweet potatoes and plantains on a sheet pan and bake for 15-20 minutes, just to dry them out a bit.
3) Meanwhile, heat 1 teaspoon of the avocado oil in a large sauté pan. Add the diced onion and sauté until translucent.
4) In a small bowl, stir together the ground chia seeds and water; allow this mixture to sit for several minutes, until it forms a "chia gel."
5) Combine sweet potato, plantain, onion, salt, pepper and chia gel in a large bowl and use your hands to mix well. Separate the mixture into ½ cup portions and form into patties.
6) Heat 1-1½ inches avocado oil in a deep sauté pan. Once the oil reaches 350°F, shallow fry each patty until golden brown.
7) Allow to drain on paper towels or over a wire rack.

TO SERVE:

1) In a medium bowl, toss mixed greens with extra virgin olive oil, lemon juice, salt and pepper.
2) Place two patties in each serving bowl and garnish with mixed baby green salad and diced avocado.
3) Add tomatillo sauce to taste.

TIP: Make a bigger batch & freeze the patties on a sheet pan for 2-3 hours before transferring them to an airtight container. When ready to make, heat 1-1½ inches of avocado oil in a deep sauté pan to 350°F. Shallow fry the desired number of patties until golden brown on each side.

SAVORY JALAPEÑO WAFFLES

MAKES 8 WAFFLES

When you want the comfort of a waffle, but not the sweetness, this will be your new go-to recipe. These are perfect for breakfast, or any time of the day. We serve these with guacamole and pico de gallo, but they also work well with eggs. If you don't have a waffle maker, you can use this batter to make delicious pancakes!

FOR THE BATTER:

1 cup / 245g Coconut Milk (p. 215) or canned
¼ cup / 52g avocado oil
3 teaspoons / 27g apple cider vinegar
3 tablespoons / 27g ground flax
¾ cup / 100g almond flour
½ cup / 60g cassava flour
1 tablespoon / 8g arrowroot flour
½ teaspoon / 4g Himalayan pink salt
½ teaspoon / 1g black pepper
1 teaspoon / 5g baking soda
2 tablespoons / 14g nutritional yeast
1 teaspoon / 2g garlic powder
1 teaspoon / 2g onion powder
1 medium / 30g jalapeño, seeded and diced small

TO SERVE:

½ cup / 85g Pico de Gallo (p. 81) or good quality store-bought
1 sliced avocado or 2 tablespoons / 40g Guacamole (p. 80)
1 tablespoon / 3g chopped cilantro

METHOD:

1) In a medium bowl, whisk together the coconut milk, avocado oil, apple cider vinegar and ground flax.

2) In a separate bowl, whisk together the remaining ingredients. Pour the dry ingredients into the wet ingredients and whisk well to combine.

3) Brush a heated waffle iron with a little bit of oil. Spoon in ¼ cup of the batter at a time and cook until browned. Continue with the remaining batter.

4) Serve with a scoop of pico de gallo, avocado or a scoop of guacamole, and a sprinkle of chopped cilantro.

BREAKFAST TACOS

SERVES 2

These tacos, filled with a smoky sweet potato hash, gooey coconut cheese, pico de gallo, guacamole, and optional scrambled eggs, are a satisfying, hearty, but not overly filling option for breakfast or any time of the day. I love them on homemade coconut flour tortillas, but if you can find our Real Coconut Grain-Free Wraps, you can use them with this recipe to make excellent breakfast burritos.

FOR THE SWEET POTATO HASH:

1 tablespoon / 14g avocado oil
½ small / 60g onion, diced very small
1 small / 100g sweet potato, peeled and diced very small
½ / 80g red bell pepper, seeded and diced very small
½ teaspoon / 1g smoked paprika
¼ teaspoon / 1g dried oregano
¼ teaspoon / 1g fresh thyme, chopped
¼ cup / 57g water
¼ teaspoon / 1g Himalayan pink salt
pinch ground black pepper
2 teaspoons / 2g chopped cilantro

FOR THE TACOS:

4 eggs (optional)
4 Coconut Flour Tortillas (p. 43) or store-bought
4 tablespoons / 60g Chipotle Coconut Cheese (p. 220)
½ medium / 68g avocado
4 tablespoons / 48g pico de gallo, (p. 81) or good quality store-bought
1 tablespoon / 6g sliced green onion

TO MAKE THE SWEET POTATO HASH:

1) In a small sauté pan, warm the avocado oil over medium heat. Add the onion and sauté until translucent.
2) Add the diced sweet potato, red bell pepper, smoked paprika, dried oregano and thyme; sauté until the sweet potato starts to brown.
3) Add water and scrape the pan to release any browned bits stuck to the bottom. Simmer until the water has evaporated and the sweet potatoes are tender. Season with salt and pepper, sprinkle in the cilantro and stir to combine.

TO MAKE THE TACOS:

1) Crack the eggs into the hash and stir to scramble.
2) In a large sauté pan, warm the tortillas lightly on both sides.
3) Fill each tortilla with the hash, chipotle cheese, avocado, pico de gallo and green onions. Eat immediately or wrap in sandwich paper for a portable treat.

TIP: Wrap the tortillas in a warm, damp kitchen towel to keep them soft and pliable after heating.

RANCHERO EGGS

SERVES 2

Most people don't think of Huevos Rancheros as a light breakfast option, but this version, made with our coconut flour tortillas and coconut cheese, homemade ranchero sauce, and lots of avocado, is just that. Not at all greasy yet incredibly satisfying, this dish is a serious crowd-pleaser. This recipe makes 2 cups of ranchero sauce, so you can easily scale up to feed a crowd; but any leftover sauce will keep in the fridge for up to a week, or in the freezer for several months.

FOR THE RANCHERO SAUCE:

8 medium/ 480g Roma tomatoes, cut in half
½ medium / 80g onion, quartered
4 cloves / 20g garlic
1 small / 15g jalapeño
2 tablespoons / 28g avocado oil
¼ cup / 12g chopped cilantro
1 teaspoon / 5g lime juice
½ teaspoon / 4g Himalayan pink salt
¼ teaspoon / 1g ground black pepper

FOR THE RANCHERO EGGS:

1 medium /120g avocado, smashed + 1 medium / 120g avocado, finely diced
2 tablespoons / 28g avocado oil + more as needed
4 coconut flour tortillas (p. 43) or store-bought
4 tablespoons / 30g Coconut Cheese (p. 219), warm
4 eggs
⅓ cup /175g ranchero sauce, warm
2 tablespoons / 15g sunflower sprouts or microgreens
½ cup / 85g pico de gallo (p. 81) or store-bought

TO MAKE THE RANCHERO SAUCE:

1) Preheat the oven to 400°F.
2) In a medium bowl, toss the tomatoes, onion, garlic, and jalapeño with avocado oil to coat. Transfer to a sheet pan with parchment or a silicone mat, making sure everything is in a single layer. Roast in the oven for 30-45 minutes, until very brown.
3) Transfer to a food processor and add cilantro, lime juice, salt and pepper. Purée until smooth; check seasoning, adding more salt and pepper to taste.

TO MAKE THE RANCHERO EGGS:

1) Divide the smashed avocado between 2 plates.
2) Heat the avocado oil in a nonstick skillet over medium flame. When hot, add 2 tortillas to the pan and cook until crisped. Repeat with the remaining 2 tortillas, adding more oil as needed.
3) Arrange the tortillas on top of the smashed avocado and spread each one with cheese.
4) Heat a little more oil in the nonstick pan and fry the eggs. Top each tortilla with a fried egg and pour warm ranchero sauce over each.
5) Garnish with finely diced avocado, sprouts and pico de gallo.

CHILAQUILES

SERVES 2

Our grain-free, dairy-free twist on a traditional Mexican dish. We replace fried corn totopos with coconut flour tortilla chips, and dairy cheese with coconut cheese. Once your tortilla chips and coconut cheese are made (or if you have our packaged Real Coconut Chips on hand), this recipe comes together in under 10 minutes. You can serve this as-is, but I always add salad greens to lighten the plate up a bit.

INGREDIENTS:

1 tablespoon / 14g avocado oil

4 eggs

1 medium / 60g Roma tomato, diced

1 large handful Coconut Tortilla Chips (p. 45)

¼ cup / 30g Coconut Cheese (p. 219), warm

2 tablespoons / 64g salsa verde - choose a natural store-bought option

1 medium / 136g avocado, sliced

chopped cilantro

METHOD:

1) Heat the avocado oil in a nonstick sauté pan over low heat.
2) Crack your eggs into the pan, stirring constantly with a rubber spatula to scramble.
3) When the eggs are halfway set, add the Roma tomatoes and tortilla chips; fold together until the chips are coated with the egg mixture.
4) Transfer to a plate and top with coconut cheese, salsa, sliced avocado, and cilantro.

EGGS BENEDICT

SERVES 2

My favorite brunch at Real Coconut! The plantain flour English muffin provides the perfect base, but if you don't have time to make these, plantain bread cut into squares also works, or even a store-bought grain-free bread. For a vegetarian version, substitute 4 tablespoons of Coconut Bacon (page 225) for the smoked salmon. I recommend saving this Hollandaise sauce recipe for future use—it's so good drizzled over a plate of asparagus or broccoli.

FOR THE HOLLANDAISE SAUCE:
1 cup / 215g avocado oil
2 egg yolks
1½ teaspoons / 7g apple cider vinegar
1½ teaspoons / 7g water
1 teaspoons / 5g lime juice
pinch Himalayan pink salt
pinch black pepper

FOR THE EGGS BENEDICT:
2 English muffins or 2 slices Plantain Bread (p. 60)
½ teaspoon / 2g apple cider vinegar
4 organic pasture-raised eggs
1 avocado, sliced
8 slices / 90g smoked salmon
6 asparagus spears, blanched
6 cherry tomatoes, halved
2 tablespoons / 20g sunflower sprouts or microgreens

TO MAKE THE HOLLANDAISE SAUCE:
1) Heat the avocado oil in a small saucepan until just warm.
2) In a blender, combine the egg yolks, apple cider vinegar, water, lime juice, salt and pepper; blend on medium speed. With the blender running, slowly drizzle in the warm avocado oil to form an emulsion.
3) Check for seasoning, adding more salt and pepper to taste; keep warm in a bain marie while you prepare the rest of the dish.

TO MAKE THE EGGS BENEDICT:
1) Cut the English muffin in half lengthwise and pop in the toaster.
2) Fill a medium saucepan with water and bring to a boil. Add the apple cider vinegar, and reduce the heat to maintain a gentle simmer.
3) Crack the eggs, one at a time, into a small bowl and carefully drop into the water.
4) Cover the pot with a lid and turn off the flame; set a timer for 4 minutes for soft yolks.
5) While the eggs poach, place the English muffin, cut side up, on a plate. Top each muffin half with sliced avocado and salmon (if using).
6) When the eggs are ready, use a slotted spoon to carefully scoop them one at a time from the poaching liquid. Allow the water to drain away and place the eggs on the smoked salmon.
7) Pour warm hollandaise sauce over the top and garnish with asparagus, cherry tomato and sprouts.

SALADS, SOUPS & LIGHT BITES

This is one of my favorite sections . . . dips, soups, an abundance of salads and more! Designed to be simple to prepare and light on the digestion, these dishes are perfect for a smaller meal or snack, or you can mix and match a few to create a full banquet! At the restaurant, we serve some salads, soups and light bites at both lunch and dinner, and always encourage people to build their perfect meal with a little of this and a little of that. I might have a mini cup of Broccoli Soup (page 102), a big Baby Kale Salad (page 95), and an order of Baked Sweet Potato Fries (page 114) one day, or share Nachos (page 109) with the table and order a Green Caesar Salad (page 96) for myself. These recipes are also great for entertaining—I'll often make six or eight of them to serve buffet- or family-style, or turn them into starters for a more formal, plated dinner party.

GUACAMOLE

MAKES 2 CUPS

My love of guacamole is one of the things that started everything. When we first moved to Mexico, I wanted to eat it with every meal but couldn't stomach the triple-fried corn tostadas that were always served with it. So in a way, my quest for a grain-free vehicle for guacamole is the main reason the coconut flour tortillas and chips were born!

Guacamole goes with almost everything and is so simple to make. If you are not already a pro, you'll soon be making it with your eyes closed. It's wonderful as a side, snack or starter (load it onto our coconut flour tortilla chips or enjoy with crudités), and also features as a component in lots of the recipes in this book. I prefer a chunkier guacamole, so I cube the avocados and then lightly mash them. The jalapeño is optional, but I love this addition in mine for a little kick.

INGREDIENTS:

¼ medium / 30g red onion, finely diced
½ bunch / 20g cilantro, chopped
1 small / 10g jalapeño, seeded and finely diced
2 tablespoons / 30g lime juice
2 medium / 300g avocados, halved, pitted, and cut into small cubes
½ teaspoon / 4g Himalayan pink salt
¼ teaspoon / 2g black pepper

METHOD:

1) In a medium bowl, combine the red onion, cilantro, jalapeño and lime juice.
2) Scoop the avocado flesh into the bowl and season with salt and pepper.
3) Using a spoon or fork, lightly mash the avocado while incorporating it into the other ingredients.

PICO DE GALLO

MAKES 2 CUPS

Literally translated as the beak of the rooster, pico de gallo is served everywhere in Mexico. While it's a refreshing and nutritious salsa on its own, the triple-fried corn tostadas that are traditionally served alongside it are definitely something to avoid. Our coconut flour tortilla chips make the perfect partner for a side in its own right, but you will also find this salsa featured in many of the other recipes in this book.

INGREDIENTS:

7 medium / 420g Roma tomatoes, seeded and finely diced
½ medium / 70g red onion, finely diced
1 small / 20g jalapeño, seeded and finely chopped
½ bunch / 20g cilantro, finely chopped
2 tablespoons / 28g lime juice
½ teaspoon / 4g Himalayan pink salt
¼ teaspoon / 2g ground black pepper

METHOD:

1) In a large bowl, mix together all ingredients. Use immediately or store in refrigerator for up to 1 day.

MAYAN TZIKIL PAK DIP

SERVES 2

When I first tasted "real" Mayan Tzikil Pak at our dear friend and Mayan elder Abuelo Antonio Oxte's home in the village of Sisbichen, I knew it had to be on our menu. The toasted pumpkin seeds, or "pepitas" as they are known in Spanish, lend a nutty flavor, which is perfectly balanced by the acidity of the tomatoes and jalapeño. Serve this warm or at room temperature with chips or crudités.

INGREDIENTS:

- 6 medium / 375g Roma tomatoes, cut in half lengthwise
- 1 small / 100g onion, roughly chopped
- 1 small / 5g jalapeño, halved and seeded
- avocado oil to coat
- ½ teaspoon / 4g Himalayan pink salt
- ¼ teaspoon / 4g black pepper
- 1 tablespoon / 5g cilantro, finely chopped
- 1 cup / 100g pumpkin seeds, toasted and ground

METHOD:

1) Preheat the oven to 350°F.
2) In a large bowl, toss the tomato halves, onion and jalapeño with enough avocado oil to coat. Transfer to a sheet pan lined with parchment paper or a silicone mat and roast in the oven until very browned (about 1 hour).
3) Remove the sheet pan from the oven and allow to cool to room temperature.
4) Once cool, transfer the mixture to a food processor. Add salt and pepper and pulse until the tomatoes are broken down, but not completely puréed.
5) Pour the sauce into a mixing bowl and stir in the cilantro and ground pumpkin seeds.

HEMP TAHINI DIP

MAKES 1 CUP M

Tahini is usually made from sesame seeds, but I think it's even better made with one of my favorite ingredients, toasted hemp. I love this with crudités, but it's also delicious spread on toast or crackers. A great make-ahead option, this dip will keep in the fridge for several weeks.

INGREDIENTS:

4 cloves / 20g garlic, peeled + 1 clove / 5g garlic, roughly chopped
1 teaspoon / 4g avocado oil
1 cup / 160g Toasted Hemp (p. 222)
2 teaspoons / 10g lemon juice
¼ teaspoon / 3g Himalayan pink salt
pinch black pepper
3 tablespoons / 42g extra virgin olive oil

METHOD:

1) Preheat the oven to 350°F.
2) Place 4 garlic cloves on a small square of aluminum foil and add the avocado oil. Pull up the sides of the foil to enclose the garlic. Roast in the oven for about 15 minutes, or until softened and browned.
3) Using a food processor, purée the toasted hemp until a paste forms. Add the roasted garlic, remaining raw garlic clove, lemon juice, salt and pepper and continue puréeing (scraping down the sides as needed), until the mixture is very smooth and shiny.
4) With the motor running, slowly drizzle in extra virgin olive oil.
5) Transfer to a bowl and serve with your favorite crudités.

SPINACH CHEESE DIP

SERVES 2   M

Our spin on a favorite (not so healthy) dip uses coconut cheese in place of the standard cream cheese, and is served with our coconut flour tortilla chips. So much lighter and easier to digest than the original, this is a dip you can devour guilt (and tummy ache!) free.

INGREDIENTS:

1 tablespoon / 14g avocado oil
½ small / 100g onion, finely diced
2 cloves / 10g garlic, minced
8 ounces / 226g frozen spinach, thawed
¼ cup / 60g Coconut Milk (p. 215) or canned
1¾ cups / 225g Coconut Cheese (p. 219)
3 tablespoons / 15g nutritional yeast
½ teaspoon / 4g Himalayan pink salt
¼ teaspoon / 1g black pepper
coconut flour tortilla chips (p. 45) or store-bought

METHOD:

1) Heat the avocado oil in a medium pan. Add the onions and sauté until translucent.
2) Add the minced garlic and sauté for another 2 minutes, then add the spinach and sauté until warmed through. Transfer to a colander and drain well.
3) Add the coconut milk and coconut cheese to the pot and cook over medium heat, stirring until the mixture is melted and smooth.
4) Add the drained spinach mixture, nutritional yeast, salt and pepper and stir to combine.
5) Serve warm with coconut flour tortilla chips.

TIP: If desired, you can spoon into a ceramic or cast iron dish and bake in a 425°F oven until browned and bubbly.

CHARRED JALAPEÑO, RADISH & PEPITA GUACAMOLE

SERVES 2 - 4

I like to think of this as guacamole's more sophisticated cousin, with a bit of a kick! This is my new favorite dip, especially when eaten with starchy, crunchy, slightly sweet plantain chips. If you want to make this extra special (maybe you're serving it to guests or maybe you just want to treat yourself!), artfully arrange the radishes, diced red onion, and chopped cilantro in lines on top of the mashed avocado.

INGREDIENTS:

2 small / 14g jalapeños
2 medium, 270g avocados
¼ teaspoon / 3g Himalayan pink salt
pinch black pepper
1 tablespoon / 14g lime juice
3 radishes, julienned
2 tablespoons / 30g finely diced red onion
2 tablespoons / 10g finely chopped cilantro
3 tablespoons / 40g pumpkin seeds, toasted

METHOD:

1) Roast the jalapeños over an open flame until charred. Allow them to cool slightly, then chop into very small pieces.

2) In a medium bowl, roughly chop or mash the avocados with the salt, pepper and lime juice. Transfer to a serving bowl.

3) Top with radish, charred jalapeño, red onion, cilantro, and pumpkin seeds; serve with plantain chips, coconut flour tortilla chips and/or crudités.

SUPER GREEN SALAD

SERVES 2

I had a vision of a salad overflowing with everything green, and this salad does just that! Use whatever goodies you can find at the supermarket (or even better, the farmers market); just pile them all in, and of course, I add avocado to almost everything! The kicky ginger vinaigrette is the perfect complement to all the grassy leaves & sprouts. Make this more substantial by adding toasted seeds (page 226) or a protein of your choice.

FOR THE GINGER VINAIGRETTE:

1 teaspoon / 5g minced ginger

¼ cup / 60g lime juice

1 teaspoon / 5g Dijon mustard

½ teaspoon / 4g Himalayan pink salt

¼ teaspoon / 3g black pepper

¾ cup / 160g avocado oil

FOR THE SALAD:

5 cups / 170g mixed baby greens (spinach, arugula, baby kale, mixed lettuces)

1 cup / 32g sunflower sprouts or microgreens

1 medium / 136g avocado, diced

METHOD:

1) To make the vinaigrette, purée all the ingredients in a blender for 2 minutes.

2) To assemble the salad, toss the mixed baby greens and sprouts or microgreens with ¼ cup of the vinaigrette (use more or less according to your preference) in a large mixing bowl.

3) Transfer to a salad plate or bowl and top with diced avocado.

RADISH & ARUGULA SALAD

SERVES 2

I've been obsessed with this salad for a while now! I love the sourness of pickles, and my obsession with greens and avocados is certainly no secret, so for me, this salad has it all. It's such an easy recipe, and the dressing keeps for what seems like forever! I often top this with some grilled shrimp when I'm in Tulum, or a cut-up boiled egg when I'm in Los Angeles.

INGREDIENTS:

1 medium / 44g shallot, finely diced
½ cup / 120g white vinegar
2 medium radishes, very thinly sliced
3 cups / 100g arugula, lightly packed
1½ cups / 50g baby spinach, lightly packed
½ cup / 15g microgreens
1 teaspoon / 8g Himalayan pink salt
½ teaspoon / 3g black pepper
½ cup / 110g extra virgin olive oil
1 medium / 160g avocado, diced
¼ cup / 40g shelled pumpkin seeds, toasted

METHOD:

1) Combine the shallot and vinegar in a small bowl and soak in the fridge overnight.
2) In a large mixing bowl, toss together the radishes, arugula, baby spinach and microgreens.
3) To make the dressing, drain ¼ cup of the shallot liquid into pint size mason jar. Add the salt, pepper and extra virgin olive oil; cover tightly with the lid and shake well.
4) Pour desired amount over the greens and toss well. Scoop the shallots out from the remaining liquid and sprinkle over the greens.
5) Garnish with avocado and toasted pumpkin seeds.

CREAMY SLAW

SERVES 2

Crunchy and satisfying, this slaw is a go-to favorite and an all round winner! It makes a nutritious side dish for something like our Roasted Cauliflower Soup (page 104), but can also be easily transformed into a meal-sized salad; just add some of your favorite leaves, cubes of avocado, and some seeds (I especially love it with black sesame).

FOR THE VEGAN RANCH DRESSING:

½ cup / 126g Coconut Yogurt (p. 49) or store-bought
2 teaspoons / 2g parsley, finely chopped
½ teaspoon / 1g chives, finely chopped
1 tablespoon / 14g lime juice
1 tablespoon / 14g apple cider vinegar
¼ teaspoon / 1g garlic powder
¼ teaspoon / 1g onion powder
¼ teaspoon / 3g Himalayan pink salt
¼ teaspoon / 1g black pepper

FOR THE SLAW:

1 cup / 70g green cabbage, thinly sliced
1 cup / 70g red cabbage, thinly sliced
1 medium carrot, grated
¼ cup / 30g red onion, very thinly sliced
1 stalk / 30g celery, very thinly sliced
cilantro to garnish

METHOD:

1) To make the dressing, simply whisk together all the ingredients; refrigerate for 30 minutes to allow the flavors to combine.
2) To assemble the slaw, combine the green and red cabbage, carrot, onion and celery in a large bowl. Toss with the vegan ranch dressing to taste.
3) Garnish with cilantro leaves and serve immediately.

BABY KALE SALAD

SERVES 2

Despite how popular kale has been for so long, I was never a fan of kale salads and never ordered them in restaurants or ate them at home. I felt like I wasn't keeping up with a major food trend, but my stomach just couldn't digest this tough and fibrous plant unless it was cooked. That was until I discovered baby kale and my eyes were opened to a whole new world of salad possibilities! Because baby kale is so much easier to digest and doesn't require any pre-prep, I'm now throwing it into salads left and right. Here, we pair it with crisp sprouts and shaved fennel, creamy avocado, crunchy toasted seeds, and a truly life-changing tahini dressing (I always keep a jar of this in my fridge for salads, crudités, anything, really). Serve this for lunch or a light dinner during the week.

FOR THE TAHINI DRESSING:

⅔ cup / 115g sesame tahini or Hemp Tahini (p. 222)

1 clove / 5g garlic

2-inch piece / 9g ginger, chopped

¼ cup / 40g apple cider vinegar

½ teaspoon / 4g Himalayan pink salt

½ teaspoon / 3g black pepper

1 tablespoon / 15g lemon juice

½ teaspoon / 2g ground coriander

1 tablespoon / 20g Dijon mustard

1 cup / 165g vegetable broth

FOR THE SALAD:

5 cups / 170g baby kale

¼ cup / 10g pea sprouts

¼ cup / 10g sunflower sprouts

1 tablespoon / 2g fennel, very thinly shaved

2 medium / 300g avocados, diced large

2 tsp / 2g cilantro sprouts

2 tablespoons / 10g toasted seeds (p. 226)

TO MAKE THE TAHINI DRESSING:

1) Combine all the ingredients in a powerful blender and purée for 2 minutes.
2) Transfer to an airtight container and store in the refrigerator for up to 4 days.

TO MAKE THE SALAD:

1) In a large mixing bowl, toss together the baby kale, sprouts, fennel and ½ cup of the tahini dressing. Divide between 2 plates or shallow bowls, or pile onto a small serving platter.
2) Garnish with avocado, cilantro sprouts, and toasted seeds.

ZEN CAESAR SALAD

SERVES 2

I love this salad! Every bite is packed full of goodness and exploding with flavor, from the crisp romaine, to the creamy green dressing, to the nutty "parmesan" sprinkles and toasted hemp seeds; the coconut bacon finishes it off to perfection! The dressing is so delicious that it's hard to resist scooping it onto bits of bread or veggie scraps before it's even made it to the salad.

Admittedly, there are a few components here, but each one is pretty quick and easy to make, and the combination of flavors really is out of this world. That being said, if you're short on time, it's still unbelievably good with just the salad ingredients and dressing. There's a reason this recipe has remained a firm staple over the years in the restaurant, and will likely be around for a long time to come.

FOR THE GREEN CAESAR DRESSING:

½ large / 80g avocado
2 tablespoons / 30g Coconut Yogurt (p. 49) or store-bought
1 small clove / 4g garlic
10 leaves / 5g baby spinach
½ tablespoon / 1g cilantro
1 teaspoon / 5g coconut aminos
1½ tablespoons / 20g avocado oil
1 tablespoon / 14g lemon juice
½ teaspoon / 4g Himalayan pink salt
½ teaspoon / 3g black pepper
2 tablespoons / 30g water

FOR THE CROUTONS:

4 (½-inch thick) slices Plantain Bread (p. 60)
avocado oil for coating
pinch Himalayan pink salt

FOR THE NUTTY PARMESAN:

4 tablespoons / 40g ground flax
6 tablespoons / 40g nutritional yeast
¼ teaspoon / 3g Himalayan pink salt

FOR THE SALAD:

4 cups / 160g chopped romaine lettuce
¼ cup / 8g pea sprouts
¼ cup / 10g sunflower sprouts
2 tablespoons / 8g pumpkin seeds, toasted
1 large / 160g avocados, large dice
¼ cup / 30g Coconut Bacon (p. 225)
¼ cup / 4g cilantro sprouts
1 tablespoon / 2g Toasted Hemp (p. 222)

TO MAKE THE DRESSING:
1) Place all ingredients in a blender and purée for 2 minutes.
2) Store in an airtight container in the fridge for up to 3 days.

TO MAKE THE CROUTONS:
1) Preheat the oven to 325°F.
2) Cut the plantain bread slices into cubes and toss with avocado oil and salt.
3) Spread out onto a sheet pan and bake for 20-25 minutes, until crunchy. Cool completely.

TO MAKE THE NUTTY PARMESAN:
1) Whisk together all of the ingredients; store in an airtight container in the fridge for up to 1 month.

TO MAKE THE SALAD:
1) In a large mixing bowl, toss together the romaine, sprouts, pumpkin seeds and ½ cup of the dressing.
2) Pile onto a salad platter and top with diced avocado, coconut bacon, cilantro sprouts and croutons.
3) Sprinkle with toasted hemp and 1 tablespoon of the nutty parmesan mixture.

BROCCOLI, PEA & AVOCADO SALAD

SERVES 2

I love the combination of warm veggies and leaves in this salad. The dish works perfectly on its own as a light meal, but if you're looking for something a bit heartier, simply add your favorite cooked protein. Every so often I get the urge to change this up a bit, but our customers plead for me not to! Feel free to play around with other veggie combos at home . . . I do!

FOR THE DRESSING:

2 tablespoons / 28g lime juice
3 tablespoons / 42g extra virgin olive oil
¼ teaspoon / 3g Himalayan pink salt
pinch black pepper

FOR THE SALAD:

½ teaspoon / 4g Himalayan pink salt
1 cup / 68g broccoli florets
1 tablespoon / 14g avocado oil
1 medium / 150g red onion, quartered
10 cherry tomatoes
¼ cup / 56g frozen peas, thawed (or shucked fresh English peas)
2 cups / 68g baby mixed lettuces
¼ cups / 8g baby sprouts (cilantro, kale, broccoli, etc.)
1 medium / 130g avocado, diced

TO MAKE THE DRESSING:

1) To make the dressing, whisk together all of the ingredients; set aside.

TO MAKE THE SALAD:

1) Fill a medium saucepan with water and bring to a boil; sprinkle in the salt. Add the broccoli and boil until just tender but still bright green; drain and set aside.
2) Heat the avocado oil in a sauté pan over medium flame. Add the red onion quarters and cook until browned and softened. Remove from the pan and set aside to cool.
3) In the same pan, sauté the cherry tomatoes until they start to blister. Remove and set aside to cool.
4) In a large bowl, toss together the broccoli, red onion, cherry tomatoes, peas, baby lettuces and baby sprouts with the dressing. Taste for seasoning and top with diced avocado.

CHARRED SWEET POTATO SALAD

SERVES 2

If you are a big fan of sweet potatoes, but looking for a fun way to switch things up, you'll love this recipe. Super easy to make, this simple salad works well as a comforting side dish, but can just as easily be paired with leafy greens and diced avocado, making it a main course feast in its own right! Slightly charring the cubes caramelizes the sugars in the sweet potato, and is key to bringing out the flavor here. Be careful not to go overboard, though, as you don't want them to burn!

FOR THE VINAIGRETTE:

1 clove / 5g garlic
1 lime, zested
¼ cup / 60g lime juice
2 tablespoons / 28g apple cider vinegar
1 teaspoon / 5g Dijon mustard
½ teaspoon / 1g ground coriander
½ teaspoon / 1g ground California chili pepper
½ teaspoon / 4g Himalayan pink salt
¼ teaspoon / 2g black pepper
1 cup / 218g avocado oil

FOR THE SALAD:

3 large / 1000g sweet potatoes, skin on and cut into 1" cubes
avocado oil to coat
1 teaspoon / 8g Himalayan pink salt
½ teaspoon / 3g black pepper
2 stalks / 60g celery, finely diced
½ small / 35g red onion, finely diced
1 tablespoon / 3g cilantro, chopped
1 tablespoon / 14g lime juice
¼ cup / 8g cilantro sprouts

TO MAKE THE VINAIGRETTE:

1) Blend all the ingredients except the avocado oil in a blender until smooth. With the blender running, slowly drizzle in the avocado oil.

TO MAKE THE SALAD:

1) Preheat the oven to 425°F.
2) In a large mixing bowl, toss the sweet potato with the avocado oil, salt and pepper. Transfer to a sheet pan and roast in the oven until tender and charred around the edges (about 20 minutes).
3) To assemble the salad, toss together the roasted sweet potatoes, diced celery, red onion and chopped cilantro in a large bowl. Drizzle over the lime juice and ⅓ cup of the vinaigrette and toss to combine.
4) Transfer to serving bowls and garnish with cilantro sprouts.

TIP: This makes extra vinaigrette, but it keeps in the fridge for about a week and is so good tossed with just about any combination of greens and veg.

AVOCADO GAZPACHO

SERVES 2 - 4

A cooling & refreshing chilled soup, this recipe has all the benefits and goodness of the avocado and spinach, and is so quick to throw together (literally toss everything in the blender). The trick here is ensuring that the soup is really well chilled before serving. It tastes best when it's nice and cold, plus letting it sit in the fridge for a couple of hours gives all of the flavors and ingredients time to infuse and marry. If you're in a rush, you can always blast it for 20 minutes in the freezer, but don't be tempted to add ice cubes (as is sometimes done with traditional gazpacho); you will compromise the creaminess, which is the big selling point of the soup!

INGREDIENTS:

2 / 320g large avocados
1 clove / 5g garlic
½ teaspoon / 1g minced ginger
1 tablespoon / 12g yellow onion, roughly chopped
1 stalk / 40g celery, roughly chopped
½ medium / 80g cucumber, peeled, seeded, and roughly chopped
1 tablespoon / 2g parsley leaves
¼ cup / 8g packed baby spinach
2 tablespoons / 30g lime juice
2 teaspoons / 16g Himalayan pink salt
½ teaspoon / 3g black pepper
½ small / 7g jalapeño, optional
3½ cups / 800g vegetable stock, chilled

METHOD:

1) Purée all ingredients in a blender. Season to taste with more salt and/or lime juice.
2) Cover and chill in the refrigerator for at least 2 hours before serving.

BROCCOLI SOUP

SERVES 2

Believe it or not, almost as many people have asked us for this recipe as the tortillas, smoothies, and sweet treats! It's such a simple dish, but there's so much goodness in it, and the deep green color makes you feel good just looking at it. I know that some of our regular guests in Tulum eat this before they go for dinner in other restaurants, just in case they don't like what's served where they are booked! My trick at the restaurant is to order a mini bowl of this with my main meal, and many friends and customers have begun to follow suit. In fact, I may need to put a mini option on the menu so that everyone can get their fix! If you're making this for guests, go the extra mile and garnish each bowl with a few pan-cooked broccoli florets and grilled onions—it transforms this humble soup into something seriously dinner party–worthy.

INGREDIENTS:

2 tablespoons / 28g avocado oil

1 medium / 150g onion, roughly chopped

3 cloves / 15g garlic, roughly chopped

½ cup / 75g green peas

5 cups / 170g baby spinach

½ medium / 100g head broccoli, cut into florets

1 medium / 136g avocado

5 ounces / 150g Coconut Milk (p. 215) or canned

1 teaspoon / 4g Himalayan pink salt

½ teaspoon / 3g black pepper

METHOD:

1) Heat the avocado oil in a saucepan over medium flame. Add the onion and sauté until translucent. Add the garlic and peas and sauté for 5 minutes. Add the spinach and broccoli and sauté for 5 more minutes.

2) Add the coconut milk, salt and pepper and bring the soup up to a light simmer, just to heat through.

3) Transfer the mixture to a blender, add the avocado and carefully blend until smooth. Pour into soup bowls and serve hot.

ROASTED CAULIFLOWER SOUP

SERVES 2

This is a comforting, warming, simple soup that works equally well in winter or summer. In the winter, enjoy it steaming hot, and in summer, just gently warm it. Roasting the cauliflower is key for the flavor—it just gives it that extra something, which is worth waiting for.

INGREDIENTS:

- ½ head / 420g of cauliflower
- 1 tablespoon / 14g avocado oil + extra for roasting
- ½ medium / 75g yellow onion, roughly chopped
- 2 cloves / 10g garlic, roughly chopped
- 2 cups / 500ml vegetable stock
- ½ teaspoon / 4g Himalayan pink salt
- ¼ teaspoon / 3g black pepper
- chopped parsley, to garnish

METHOD:

1) Preheat the oven to 350°F.
2) Cut the cauliflower into florets and toss with a little avocado oil to lightly coat.
3) Line 2 sheet pans with parchment paper and spread the cauliflower out in a single layer. Roast in the oven for 30-40 minutes, until dark golden brown.
4) In a large saucepan, heat the tablespoon of avocado oil over low flame. Add the onion and sauté until translucent. Add the garlic and sauté for 2 minutes. Add the roasted cauliflower, vegetable stock, salt and pepper, and stir to lift any pieces of onion or garlic that may have stuck to the bottom of the pot.
5) Bring the mixture to a boil, then reduce the heat to low and cover. Simmer for 10-15 minutes or until the cauliflower is very tender.
6) Remove from the heat and transfer contents to a blender; purée until very smooth. If the mixture is too thick, thin it out with a little more vegetable stock.
7) Divide the soup between 2 bowls and serve with a sprinkle of chopped parsley.

GOLDEN BROTH

SERVES 2 E

This soothing, hearty soup is an anti-inflammatory delight, brimming with all sorts of goodness! Make it vegan by using vegetable broth, and loading up with more veggies instead of chicken. The broth base also works well as a "sipping soup"—just pour it into a mug or travel cup, and enjoy on the go. If you have broth on hand or in the freezer, this is a quick and easy meal to make.

INGREDIENTS:

½ cup / 60g sweet potato, 1½ inch dice

1 teaspoon / 4g + 1 tablespoon / 14g avocado oil

4 teaspoons / 28g green or yellow curry paste (we like Thai Kitchen brand)

1 teaspoon / 2g turmeric root, grated

1 teaspoon / 2g ginger, grated

3 cups / 380g chicken broth

½ cup / 16g baby kale

½ cup / 80g shredded roasted chicken

1 cup / 225g Coconut Milk (p. 215) or canned

½ teaspoon / 4g Himalayan pink salt

½ teaspoon / 3g black pepper

1 lime, juiced and zested

small handful / 6g of cilantro leaves

METHOD:

1) Preheat the oven to 400°F.

2) Toss the sweet potato pieces with 1 teaspoon of avocado oil to coat. Place in a small square of aluminum foil and fold up the sides to make a pouch.

3) Roast in the oven until tender (about 15 minutes). Open the foil packet and continue roasting for another 10 minutes, or until browned.

4) Meanwhile, heat the remaining tablespoon of avocado oil in a small saucepan. Add the curry paste, turmeric, and ginger and sauté for 2 minutes. Add a splash of chicken broth if the mixture is looking too dry.

5) Add the chicken broth and simmer on low heat for 5 minutes. Add the sweet potato, baby kale, shredded chicken and coconut milk. Bring the mixture up to a simmer and season with salt and pepper. Remove from heat and stir in the lime juice.

6) Pour into bowls and garnish with cilantro leaves and lime zest.

SOPA DE LIMA

SERVES 2 M

Sopa de Lima, or Lime Soup, is such a staple in Mexico, and for good reason! The clean brothy base, made bright and tart from tons of lime juice, is topped with sliced radishes, spicy jalapeño, creamy avocado, some shredded chicken for protein, and some crispy tortilla strips for crunch. It's the perfect thing to eat when you're feeling under the weather, or just want something soothing yet refreshing to enjoy. Often served in restaurants with the broth base, and each component in a little bowl for the customer to add in themselves (or assembled at the table), this recipe works well for entertaining, but is also easy enough to whip up for a weeknight meal. Keep the tortilla strips aside to add at the last minute so that they keep their crunch for longer.

FOR THE TORTILLA STRIPS:

2 Coconut Flour Tortillas (p. 43) or store-bought
avocado oil for frying

FOR THE SOUP:

4 cups / 1000ml chicken or vegetable broth
1 teaspoon / 8g Himalayan pink salt
½ teaspoon / 6g black pepper
1 cup / 160g cooked chicken, shredded (optional)
4 tablespoons / 50g lime juice
1 small / 10g jalapeño, thinly sliced (optional)
4 medium / 30g radishes, thinly sliced
small handful / 1g of cilantro leaves
2 teaspoons / 1g cilantro sprouts
1 large / 160g avocado, diced
2 lime wedges

TO MAKE THE TORTILLA STRIPS:

1) In a deep skillet, heat 1-1 ½ inches of avocado oil to 350°F.
2) Cut each tortilla into ¼-inch strips.
3) Scatter the strips into the oil and fry until golden brown.
4) Drain on a wire rack or over paper towels.

TO MAKE THE SOUP:

1) In a small saucepan, heat the broth, salt and pepper over medium flame. Add the shredded chicken and bring the mixture up to a boil. Turn off the heat and stir in the lime juice.
2) Transfer into a soup bowl and top with jalapeño, radish, cilantro leaves, sprouts and avocado.
3) Add the tortilla strips and serve with lime wedges on the side.

NACHOS

SERVES 2

If you've given up grains and dairy, you may think the cheesy, crunchy joy of nachos is a thing of your past. Think again! This magic recipe gives you all the salty, satisfying crunch of the Tex-Mex classic without all the heaviness and grease.

INGREDIENTS:

2 handfuls Coconut Flour Tortilla Chips (p. 45) or store-bought
1 cup / 280g Nacho Coconut Cheese (p. 221)
½ cup / 85g Pico de Gallo (p. 81) or store-bought
½ cup / 120g Guacamole (p. 80) or store-bought
2 tablespoons / 24g Coconut Sour Cream (p. 217)
1 small / 10g jalapeño, thinly sliced
1 tablespoon / 10g chopped cilantro

METHOD:

1) Preheat the oven to 350°F.
2) Place the chips in an oven-proof dish and pour the nacho cheese over the top. Bake for 10 minutes, until the cheese is lightly browned and bubbly.
3) Remove the dish from the oven and top with pico de gallo, guacamole and sour cream. Garnish with jalapeño and cilantro.

YUCCA CROQUETTES

SERVES 2

These croquettes are simply divine, and so much lighter than a traditional potato version. Stuffed with our gooey coconut cheese and basil, you won't even miss the typical dairy filling. They do take a little time to prepare, so I definitely suggest making a bigger batch and freezing. You'll get serious kitchen cred if you serve these for a get-together lunch or dinner party!

FOR THE CROQUETTES:

1 medium / 450g cassava (yucca) root, peeled
¼ teaspoon / 3g Himalayan pink salt
pinch black pepper
1 tablespoon / 25g Coconut Milk (p. 215) or canned
½ cup / 56g Coconut Cheese (p. 219)
6 small leaves of basil
½ cup / 120g Coconut Milk (p. 215) or canned
½ teaspoon / 3g apple cider vinegar
½ teaspoon / 3g lemon juice
¼ teaspoon / 1g Dijon mustard
pinch ground sage
pinch ground thyme
pinch onion powder
⅓ cup / 40g tapioca flour
¼ cup / 28g coconut flour

FOR THE TOMATO SAUCE:

1 tablespoon / 14g avocado oil
1 cup / 150g cherry tomatoes
1 clove / 5g garlic, minced
¼ teaspoon / 3g Himalayan pink salt
pinch black pepper
1 tablespoon basil, torn into small pieces

TO SERVE:

avocado oil for frying

TO MAKE THE CROQUETTES:

1) Cut the peeled yucca into 2- to 3-inch pieces crosswise. Place in a medium pot and cover with water. Bring to a boil and cook until the yucca is fork tender. Remove the yucca from the water and set aside until it is cool enough to handle.
2) Mash the yucca until mostly smooth (some small chunks are ok), then add salt, pepper and the tablespoon of coconut milk.
3) Separate into 12 equal balls about the size of a golf ball. Flatten each ball slightly and fill with about ½ teaspoon coconut cheese and half a leaf of basil, then re-form each one into a ball.
4) Whisk together the coconut milk, apple cider vinegar, lemon juice, Dijon, sage, thyme and onion powder to make a buttermilk. Set aside.
5) In a separate bowl, whisk together the tapioca flour and coconut flour to make a crumb coating. Set aside.
6) Moisten the croquettes lightly with the coconut buttermilk, then dip each one in the crumb coating. Set in the fridge for at least 1 hour.

TO MAKE THE SAUCE:

1) Heat the avocado oil in a large sauté pan. Add the cherry tomatoes and allow to blister.
2) Add the garlic and start mashing the tomatoes with the back of a wooden spoon. Add salt, pepper and basil and allow to cook until the tomatoes are very soft.

TO SERVE:

1) In a medium, high-sided pan, heat about 2 inches of avocado oil to 350°F.
2) Add 3-4 croquettes at a time and fry for about 5 minutes, rotating as needed to ensure they brown evenly. Drain on a wire rack or paper towels.
3) Serve immediately with warm cherry tomato sauce.

TIP: These can easily be made ahead, frozen, and reheated as needed. Simply lay them out in a single layer to freeze and then transfer to an airtight container to store. When ready to eat, preheat your oven to 325°F, place the frozen croquettes on a sheet pan, and bake for 10-12 minutes, or until heated through.

BARBECUE TOSTADAS

SERVES 2

These barbecue tostadas have got it all—they're a little sweet from the BBQ sauce, a little crunchy from the tostada, and a little fresh from the microgreens and avocado. The fried tostada base is insanely good, but when I'm craving something a little lighter, I swap them out for pan-toasted coconut flour tortillas, lettuce shells, or even sliced jicama. Make these vegan by using dehydrated jackfruit instead of chicken.

INGREDIENTS:

2 Coconut Flour Tortillas (p. 43) or store-bought
avocado oil for frying
1 / 200g organic, pasture-raised chicken breast or 2 thighs, or 2 cups / 170g dehydrated jackfruit
1 teaspoon / 4g avocado oil
pinch dried thyme
pinch Himalayan pink salt
pinch black pepper
small handful / 28g sliced red onion
¼ cup / 70g BBQ Sauce (p. 234) or store-bought
½ medium / 65g avocado, diced
2 teaspoons / 15g chopped cilantro
microgreens

METHOD:

1) In a medium sauté pan, heat ½-inch of avocado oil to 350°F.
2) Fry the tortillas until golden brown on both sides, flipping once while they cook.
3) Remove the tostadas from the oil and drain on a wire rack or paper towels. Set aside.
4) Preheat the oven to 400°F.
5) Toss the chicken with 1 teaspoon of avocado oil, the dried thyme, salt and pepper to coat.
6) Transfer to a sheet pan lined with parchment paper or a silicone mat and roast in the oven for 20-30 minutes, or until cooked through. Remove from the oven and let cool.
7) When the chicken is cool enough to handle, shred it with your fingers, and toss with the red onion and half of the BBQ sauce (if using jackfruit, simply substitute the jackfruit for the cooked chicken in this step).
8) Spread the other half of the BBQ sauce over each tostada, top with the chicken mixture, and place on a sheet pan. Transfer to the oven and toast for about 5-10 minutes.
9) Finish with avocado, chopped cilantro and microgreens.

BAKED SWEET POTATO FRIES

SERVES 2

I can almost guarantee that these comforting baked fries will become a new household favorite. Crunchy from the arrowroot and a little smoky from the paprika, they make a nourishing addition to so many dishes, and really round out a simple meal like salad or soup. For the record, they're also delicious on their own, simply dunked in a little BBQ Sauce (page 234), Ketchup (page 233), or Vegan Mayo (page 230).

INGREDIENTS:

- 2 small sweet potatoes
- 1 tablespoon / 8g arrowroot starch
- 2 tablespoons / 28g avocado oil
- 1 teaspoon / 3g paprika
- ¼ teaspoon / 3g Himalayan pink salt
- pinch black pepper

METHOD:

1) Preheat the oven to 450°F.
2) Wash and scrub the sweet potatoes, then cut into ¼-inch sticks, approximately 3 to 4 inches long.
3) Pat the fries dry with a clean towel, toss with the arrowroot, and coat with avocado oil. Sprinkle with paprika, salt and pepper.
4) Line a sheet pan with parchment paper and lay the fries out in a single layer, being sure not to crowd them. Bake in the oven for 20 minutes.
5) Using a wide spatula, flip the fries, making sure they are still not crowded or overlapping. Return the sheet pan to the oven and bake for another 10-15 minutes, or until crispy.

BAKED SWEET POTATO FRIES & YUCCA FRIES

YUCCA FRIES

SERVES 2   E

Cassava, also known as yucca, is a great alternative to potatoes; just be sure to remove its fibrous core to ensure a nice smooth texture. Although yucca can be baked, the root is high in starch, so these taste way better shallow fried. These fries work perfectly in our Fish & Chips recipe (page 131), but are also delicious served simply with Ketchup (page 233) or Vegan Mayo (page 230).

INGREDIENTS:

2 medium cassava (yucca) roots
avocado oil for frying
Himalayan pink salt to taste
black pepper to taste

METHOD:

1) Peel the cassava and cut into 2- to 3-inch pieces crosswise.
2) Place in a large saucepan with cold water and bring to a boil. Salt the pot generously, and continue to boil until the cassava is tender.
3) Strain, run under cold water to cool, then cut each piece into quarters lengthwise. Carefully cut out the inner fibrous core of each cassava wedge, then cut into ½-inch sticks.
4) In a deep skillet, heat 1-1½ inches of avocado oil to 350°F.
5) Shallow fry small amounts of the cassava at a time until golden brown, making sure to not overcrowd the pan.
6) Drain on a wire rack or paper towels, and season to taste with salt and pepper.

HEMP FALAFEL

MAKES 12 FALAFEL BALLS

When I lived in Egypt, I loved eating falafel, but my tummy didn't! Here, the base is comprised of plantain and sweet potato, making these falafel much easier to digest than a traditional garbanzo option. The addition of toasted hemp tahini also adds a welcome protein boost! A plant-based, protein-packed bite, these make an excellent addition to any number of dishes, or as a light bite, served with the roasted tomato chutney. They also freeze beautifully, so it's worth making a double batch.

FOR THE CHUTNEY:

4 medium / 240g Roma tomatoes, quartered
1 tablespoon / 14g avocado oil
½ medium / 60g onion, roughly chopped
1 medium / 60g carrot, roughly chopped
1 clove / 5g garlic, crushed
2 tablespoons / 30g apple cider vinegar
1 tablespoon / 15g lime juice
¼ teaspoon / 1g ground cinnamon
2 teaspoons / 8g coconut sugar
½ teaspoon / 4g Himalayan pink salt
¼ teaspoon / 1g black pepper

FOR THE FALAFEL:

1 teaspoon / 5g ground chia seeds
5 teaspoons / 25g water
2 cups / 200g grated green plantain
2 cups / 200g grated sweet potato
¼ cup / 70g hemp tahini (p. 222)
4-inch piece / 30g ginger, grated
½ cup / 12g cilantro, chopped
¼ cup / 38g coconut aminos
1 tablespoon / 5g lime juice
1 teaspoon / 8g Himalayan pink salt
½ teaspoon / 3g black pepper
4½ tablespoons / 40g cassava flour
avocado oil for frying

TO MAKE THE CHUTNEY:

1) Preheat the oven to 350°F. Place the quartered tomatoes on a sheet pan lined with parchment or a silicone mat and roast for 35-45 minutes, until soft and browned.
2) Heat the avocado oil in a saucepan over medium heat. Add the onions and carrots and sauté until onions are translucent. Add the garlic and sauté for 1 minute. Add the vinegar, lime juice, cinnamon, coconut sugar, tomatoes, salt and pepper. Simmer until the mixture thickens (about 15-20 minutes), stirring occasionally.
3) Transfer to a food processor and pulse until chunky.

TO MAKE THE FALAFEL:

1) In a small bowl stir together the chia and water; allow to sit for 5 minutes to form a "chia gel."
2) In a large bowl, mix together the plantain, sweet potato, chia gel, hemp tahini, ginger, cilantro, coconut aminos, lime juice, salt and pepper.
3) Stir in the cassava flour and form the mixture into 12 walnut-size balls.
4) Pour enough avocado oil into a deep, high-sided skillet so that it comes 1-1½ inches up the sides; heat to 325°F.
5) Add the falafel balls and shallow fry until golden brown on all sides, turning as needed.
6) Transfer to a wire rack or a paper towel–lined plate to drain and sprinkle with an extra bit of salt and pepper. Serve with the roasted tomato chutney.

PLATES

You'll find some of the cult favorites from the Real Coconut in this section, like our tacos, quesadillas, and famous chicken bites, plus grain-free pizzas! Because I'm big on customization, almost all of the dishes here that have a protein choice can be made with either fish, chicken, or a vegan substitute (either seasonal veggies or jackfruit); tacos can be served on homemade coconut flour tortillas, our packaged tortillas, or even lettuce wraps for a lighter option. In general, this section contains our more filling recipes, so I always make a point of serving them with tons of leafy greens and/or vegetables on the side (or piled right on top!). A holistic doctor once told me that if you fill up on salad to start, you'll be less likely to overeat the rest of your meal, so I always load my plate of gooey Green Tomatillo Enchiladas (page 142) or my favorite Fish & Chips (page 131) with fresh, crunchy vegetables and big leafy salads, too.

QUESADILLAS

SERVES 2

If you hear grain-free, dairy-free quesadilla and think "what's the point?" you're certainly not alone. But I bet you haven't tried this grain-free, dairy-free quesadilla yet. This is the same quesadilla recipe that I first served to my friends soon after we moved to Mexico! I thought they were being nice when they said they loved them, but it turns out they weren't alone, as these remain one of our definitive menu items that set us apart from every other restaurant. Turns out grain-free coconut flour tortillas combined with coconut cheese is still revolutionary, even after all these years! Infinitely adaptable (try filling them with tomato and basil, spinach, chicken, or shrimp!), they're also incredibly quick and easy to throw together once you've got the tortillas and coconut cheese made.

INGREDIENTS:

6 Coconut Flour Tortillas (p. 43) or store-bought
½ cup / 105g Coconut Cheese (p. 219)
1 tablespoon / 14g avocado oil
½ cup / 120g Guacamole (p. 80) or store-bought
½ cup / 85g Pico de Gallo (p. 81) or store-bought

METHOD:

1) Heat each tortilla lightly in a sauté pan.
2) Spread a heaping tablespoon of coconut cheese on each tortilla and fold in half to make half moons.
3) Heat the avocado oil in a large sauté pan over medium flame. Place the quesadillas in the pan and cook until the tortillas are browned and the cheese is melted.
4) Serve with pico de gallo and guacamole.

COCONUT CEVICHE

SERVES 2

Sun, sea, and ceviche! It's what many people come to Tulum for—to sit on our deck and enjoy a refreshingly cool, crisp ceviche, while looking out at the ocean. If you can't get to Tulum, you can bring a bit of the seaside vibe to you with this recipe. Ceviche—a seafood dish originating from Peru, in which the fish or seafood delicately "cooks" by marinating in lime juice for a few minutes—is extremely popular in Mexico. The quality of the ingredients is key here, so get the freshest fish possible; you won't be sorry. Our ceviche uses coconut milk to soften the acidity of the marinade, and passion fruit juice or pulp lends a dash of tropical flavor (though it works perfectly well if you can't get hold of this). You can also use shrimp or your other favorite seafood, or even switch out the fish for mushrooms. Any way you choose to make it, our coconut flour tortilla chips are the perfect accompaniment.

INGREDIENTS:

1 pound / 450g wild red snapper or Pacific rockfish (or 1 cup / 70g sliced button & 1 cup / 70g sliced oyster mushrooms)
1 teaspoon / 4g lime juice
1 teaspoon / 8g Himalayan pink salt
1 teaspoon / 6g black pepper
4 tablespoons / 60g Coconut Milk (p. 215) or canned
1 teaspoon / 2g grated ginger
4 teaspoons / 30g passion fruit pulp
1 small / 14g jalapeño, sliced
4 tablespoons / 12g chopped cilantro
4 small / 8g radishes, thinly sliced
½ medium / 70g avocado, diced small
2 tablespoons / 6g cilantro sprouts

METHOD:

1) Combine the fish, lime juice, salt and pepper in a medium bowl; marinate for 6 minutes. Add the coconut milk, ginger, and passion fruit pulp and check seasoning. Add the sliced jalapeño, cilantro and radishes and stir to combine.

2) Transfer to a serving bowl and top with diced avocado. Garnish with cilantro sprouts and serve with coconut flour chips.

AL PASTOR TACOS

SERVES 2

Al pastor, which means "shepherd style" in Spanish, is a popular dish brought over to central Mexico by Lebanese immigrants. Inspired by shwarma, the dish features pork marinated in a combination of smoky chile paste and sweet, tropical pineapple, then cooked on a vertical spit called a "trompo." For our Real Coconut version, we swap in shrimp or jackfruit (we think it works even better than the pork!) and sauté in a hot pan in lieu of spit-roasting. The result is a much simpler, but equally delicious, taco that has been a firm favorite in Tulum since we opened our doors back in 2015.

FOR THE MARINADE:
2 tablespoons / 28g avocado oil
8 cloves / 45g garlic, roughly chopped
8 large / 20g seeded guajillo chile pods
½ medium / 120g pineapple, center core removed, roughly chopped
⅔ cups / 150ml white wine or vegetable broth
⅔ cups / 150ml orange juice
½ teaspoon / 4g Himalayan pink salt
½ teaspoon / 3g black pepper

FOR THE TACOS:
12 shrimp, 16/20 count or 2 cups / 170g dehydrated jackfruit
¼ cup / 70g al pastor marinade
2 teaspoons / 9g avocado oil
½ teaspoon / 4g Himalayan pink salt
¼ teaspoon / 2g black pepper
6 Coconut Flour Tortillas (p. 43) or store-bought
2 tablespoons / 25g red onion, julienned
4 tablespoons / 60g pineapple, finely diced
2 tablespoons / 5g cilantro sprouts
⅓ cup / 130g Guacamole (p. 80)

TO MAKE THE MARINADE:
1) In a medium saucepan, heat the avocado oil over low flame. Add the garlic and guajillo chiles, and sauté until the garlic is lightly browned.
2) Add the pineapple and cook for 2 minutes. Add the white wine and turn the heat up to medium; let the mixture cook until it's reduced by half. Add the orange juice and reduce by half again.
3) Season with salt and pepper, transfer to a blender, and blend until completely smooth.

TO MAKE THE TACOS:
1) Toss the shrimp with ¼ cup of the marinade to coat.
2) Heat the avocado oil in a medium sauté pan. Add the marinated shrimp, season with salt and pepper, and cook over medium flame for about 3 minutes per side. If using jackfruit, simply toss it with the marinade and warm the mixture through in the pan.
3) Gently warm the tortillas in another sauté pan, and keep them warm in a damp cloth until ready to use.
4) To serve, spoon two pieces of shrimp (or ½ cup of jackfruit) onto each tortilla. Top with red onion, pineapple, and sprouts, and serve with guacamole.

FISH TACOS

SERVES 2 M

A classic Real Coconut favorite, these fish tacos have been on the menu since day one. Our guests are always raving about how well the bright, herby marinade in the fish pairs with our homemade tortillas (which, right at the start, I didn't even tell anyone were made from coconut flour; I just said it was our secret recipe if they asked!). With coconut flour tortillas on hand (either homemade or store-bought), this is a simple dish to put together. Get the best-quality fish you can source—it makes a big difference.

FOR THE MARINADE:
- ½ bunch / 20g cilantro
- ½ bunch / 20g parsley
- 2 cloves / 10g garlic
- 1 teaspoon / 1g fresh thyme
- 1 teaspoon / 2g fresh ginger, roughly chopped
- 1 stalk / 10g lemongrass, roughly chopped
- 1 teaspoon / 1g fresh oregano
- 1 teaspoon / 2g ground coriander
- 1 teaspoon / 3g black pepper
- 1½ stalks / 50g celery, roughly chopped
- ½ cup / 100g avocado oil

FOR THE TACOS:
- 12 ounces / 340g wild snapper or Pacific rockfish, skinned, filleted, and cut into 3-inch strips
- ½ teaspoon / 4g Himalayan pink salt
- 6 Coconut Flour Tortillas (p. 43) or store-bought
- microgreens, to garnish
- Guacamole (p. 80) and Pico de Gallo (p. 81) or store bought, to serve

METHOD:

1) Preheat the oven to 400°F.
2) Purée all the marinade ingredients in a blender until smooth. Coat the fish in the marinade and let sit at room temperature for 5 minutes.
3) Transfer to a sheet pan lined with parchment paper or a silicone mat and sprinkle with salt. Bake for about 10-12 minutes, until fish is firm and cooked through.
4) Arrange the fish on the tortillas, garnish with microgreens and serve with guacamole and pico de gallo.

TIP: For a vegan option, substitute your favorite roasted veggies. Cremini mushrooms, zucchini and asparagus work great! The marinade freezes well with or without the fish.

BAJA TACOS

SERVES 2 M

Baja fish tacos are arguably the tastiest of all tacos, but thanks to the heavy batter and unstable frying oil used in most restaurants and recipes, I hardly ever got to eat them! Good news for fellow fish taco fanatics: in this cleaned-up version, we dredge red snapper or rockfish in a light, grain-free batter and shallow fry in avocado oil. The result is a crunchy, salty, better-for-you fish taco that, while still a treat, won't leave you feeling heavy or uncomfortable. If you are looking for a vegan alternative, try substituting asparagus, mushrooms and/or your favorite squash for the fish.

FOR THE BATTER:

2 cups / 244g tapioca flour

⅓ cup / 37g coconut flour

2 teaspoons / 9g baking soda

1 teaspoon / 8g Himalayan pink salt

1 teaspoon / 6g black pepper

2 teaspoons / 10g lime juice

1½ cups / 360g sparkling water

FOR THE TACOS:

avocado oil for frying

½ pound / 225g skinless red snapper or Pacific rockfish, cut into 3-inch strips

6 Coconut Flour Tortillas (p. 43) or store-bought

1 cup / 70g shredded cabbage

1 cup / 170g Pico de Gallo (p. 81) or store-bought

1 cup / 238g Guacamole (p. 80) or store-bought

¼ cup / 58g Baja Mayo (p. 232)

Himalayan pink salt

black pepper

TO MAKE THE BATTER:

1) Place the dry ingredients in a medium bowl and whisk to combine. Add the wet ingredients and whisk until smooth.

TO MAKE THE TACOS:

1) In a deep sauté pan, heat 1-1½ inches of avocado oil to 350°F.

2) Dip half of the fish pieces, one at a time, into the prepared batter and carefully lower them into the hot oil, making sure they don't stick together. Fry for about 5-6 minutes, or until golden brown on both sides, flipping once.

3) Remove the fish from the oil and place on a wire rack or paper towel-lined plate to drain; sprinkle with salt and pepper. Repeat with the second half of the fish pieces.

4) Gently warm the tortillas in a sauté pan, and divide them between two plates. Fill each tortilla with cabbage, fish, pico de gallo and guacamole. Serve with Baja mayo.

A TACOS

2

This flavorful, earthy tinga sauce can be used in several dishes, but works especially well on these tacos. The incredible depth of the flavor comes from the mix of chiles and spices and combines beautifully with other classics such as pico de gallo, guacamole or avocado, and even salad leaves. Feel free to lower or raise the spice level depending on your preference, and mix it up with chicken, jackfruit or roasted vegetables. The trick with the chicken or jackfruit is to shred it very finely, which makes the texture super creamy.

FOR THE TINGA:

2 tablespoons / 28g avocado oil
½ pound / 225g pasture-raised, boneless, skinless chicken thighs or breasts
or 2 cups / 170g dried jackfruit
¼ teaspoon / 1g Himalayan pink salt
pinch black pepper
2 large / 8g guajillo chiles (dried), seeded
½ medium / 100g onion, roughly chopped
2 stalks / 100g celery, roughly chopped
1 tablespoon / 6g smoked paprika
3 cloves / 15g garlic, roughly chopped
1-inch piece / 10g ginger, roughly chopped
1 small / 5g seeded jalapeño, roughly chopped
6 medium / 360g Roma tomatoes, roughly chopped
1 teaspoon / 8g Himalayan pink salt
½ teaspoon / 3g black pepper
2 cups / 460g Chicken Broth (p. 237)

FOR THE TACOS:

6 Coconut Flour Tortillas (p. 43) or store-bought
½ cup / 35g sliced cabbage
⅓ cup / 96g Chipotle Coconut Cheese, warm (p. 220)
⅓ cup / 58g Pico de Gallo (p. 81)
¼ cup / 8g microgreens
½ avocado, cubed
2 radishes, thinly sliced

METHOD:

1) Preheat the oven to 350°F.
2) In a medium Dutch oven, heat the avocado oil over medium-high flame. Season the chicken with salt and pepper, and sear it in the pot until browned on both sides; remove and set aside. (If using jackfruit, see step 5.)
3) Add a bit more avocado oil if needed and sauté the guajillo chiles, onion, celery, and smoked paprika until lightly browned. Add the garlic, ginger, and jalapeño, and continue cooking until everything is well caramelized.
4) Add the tomatoes and cook until very soft, about 15-20 minutes. Add salt, pepper, and chicken broth, and bring the mixture up to a boil. Add the seared chicken and reduce the heat to maintain a gentle simmer.
5) Cover and place in the oven. Cook for 30-40 minutes, until the chicken is cooked through. (If using jackfruit, add the dehydrated jackfruit to the sauce and cook for 15-20 minutes.)
6) Remove the pot from the oven, scoop out the chicken, and let sit until it is cool enough to handle.
7) Return the pot to the stove and simmer over low heat for an additional 20-30 minutes until the sauce is reduced by half.
8) Transfer the sauce to a blender, purée until smooth, and return to the pot over medium flame. Use your fingers to shred the chicken and simmer in the sauce to reheat.
9) In a nonstick sauté pan, warm the tortillas lightly on both sides.
10) Top with cabbage, shredded chicken, chipotle cheese, pico de gallo, microgreens, avocado and radish.

FISH & CHIPS

SERVES 2

Being English, I found that Fish & Chips was one of the dishes I missed most after giving up grains and moving to Mexico. Thank goodness the brilliant kitchen team at the Real Coconut came up with this recipe—it not only passes the test as a replacement for the traditional greasy fish & chips, it's even better! Yucca, also known as cassava, works perfectly as a lighter and easier-to-digest alternative to the classic potato fries (or chips, as we call them in the UK).

INGREDIENTS:

1½ cups / 325g avocado oil
1 recipe fried fish batter (from Baja Taco p. 127)
12 ounces / 340g wild cod, cut into 3- to 4-inch pieces
pinch Himalayan pink salt
pinch black pepper
2 tablespoons / 8g chopped parsley
1 recipe Yucca Fries (p. 116)
¼ cup / 60g Ketchup (p. 233) or store-bought
¼ cup / 60g Vegan Mayo (p. 230) or store-bought

METHOD:

1) In a medium saucepan, heat avocado oil to 350°F.
2) Dip the cod pieces in the batter, making sure to coat all sides. Gently drop the fish into the avocado oil, 2 pieces at a time (be sure to give them enough space so they don't stick together), and fry for about 5 minutes, until golden brown.
3) Remove the fish from the oil and place on a wire rack or paper towel–lined plate to drain; sprinkle with salt, pepper and parsley.
4) Serve hot with yucca fries, ketchup, and mayo for dipping.

CRUMBED CHICKEN BITES

SERVES 2

I'd argue that these chicken bites are better than any fast food options out there and are certainly healthier! They're one of the top five recipes in our restaurants, plus my son Kai's go-to treat choice whenever he is in Tulum! If you want a lighter option, these can be baked instead of shallow fried; just dunk the chicken back in the coconut milk mixture after the initial dredge, coat in crumbled coconut flour tortilla chips (our packaged chips work best), and bake in a 350°F oven for 10-15 minutes. These work brilliantly with our Ketchup (page 233) or BBQ Sauce (page 234).

INGREDIENTS:

32 ounces / 900g Coconut Milk (p. 215) or canned
2 tablespoons / 28g apple cider vinegar
2 tablespoons / 28g lemon juice
1 tablespoon / 17g Dijon mustard
1 teaspoon / 2g ground sage
1 teaspoon / 2g ground thyme
1 teaspoon / 2g onion powder
5 pieces / 285g pasture-raised chicken breast tenders, cut in half crosswise
avocado oil for frying
⅔ cup / 80g tapioca flour
⅓ cup / 36g coconut flour
Himalayan pink salt
black pepper

METHOD:

1) Whisk together the coconut milk, apple cider vinegar, lemon juice, mustard, sage, thyme, and onion powder. Submerge the chicken pieces in the mixture and place in the fridge overnight (or at least several hours) to marinate.

2) Pour 1 -1½ inches of avocado oil into a deep skillet. Heat to 325°F, and remove the marinated chicken from the fridge.

3) In a shallow dish, whisk together the tapioca flour and coconut flour. Pull the chicken from the marinade and dip into the flour mixture, making sure to coat evenly.

4) Carefully place the chicken into the avocado oil and fry until golden brown on all sides, about 5 minutes. Using tongs or a slotted spoon, drain the bites on a wire rack or over paper towels.

5) Sprinkle with salt and pepper and serve with BBQ sauce or ketchup.

NACHO BOWL

SERVES 2

I love how this nacho bowl provides the best of both worlds—you've got the big, healthy salad base plus the slightly indulgent combo of saucy chicken, chips, sour cream, and chipotle coconut cheese! It's a visual delight too . . . the salad leaves and microgreens, avocado, and pico de gallo contrast so well with the tinga and chipotle cheese.

For a vegan option, substitute 1½ cups / 125g packed dehydrated jackfruit (from Barbecue Tostadas recipe, page 113) or your favorite veggies.

INGREDIENTS:

12 large handfuls mixed baby greens
1 recipe chicken tinga (from Tinga Tacos, p. 128)
1 cup / 250g Chipotle Coconut Cheese, warmed (p. 220)
2 handfuls of Coconut Flour Tortilla Chips (p. 45) or store-bought (Original flavor)
¼ cup / 56g Coconut Sour Cream (p. 217)
1 cup / 170g Pico de Gallo (p. 81) or store-bought
½ cup / 120g Guacamole (p. 80) or store-bought
¼ cup / 8g microgreens or sunflower sprouts

METHOD:

1) Divide the salad greens between two shallow bowls.
2) Top with chicken tinga, chipotle cheese, chips, coconut sour cream, pico de gallo, guacamole and microgreens.

BURRITO BOWL

MAKES 1 BOWL

I'd argue that this deconstructed burrito bowl is even better than a traditional burrito for lots of reasons. First, you can really see and appreciate all the components. Second, you'll get more of the good stuff (cauliflower rice, mixed greens, etc). Third, you'll inevitably end up not over-full. This bowl works at any time of the day; change up the base recipe by adding eggs for a breakfast-style burrito bowl, or shredded chicken or toasted hemp for an added protein boost.

FOR THE CAULIFLOWER RICE:
½ medium head / 300g cauliflower
2 tablespoons avocado oil
1 medium / 150g onion, diced small
2 teaspoons / 5g minced garlic
½ teaspoon / 4g Himalayan pink salt
¼ teaspoon / 2g black pepper
½ cup / 64g vegetable stock
¼ cup / 16g chopped cilantro
zest and juice of 1 lime

FOR THE BOWLS:
2 tablespoons / 28g avocado oil, divided
¼ small / 30g yellow onion, thinly sliced
1 clove / 5g garlic, minced
½ medium / 80g red bell pepper, thinly sliced
½ medium / 80g yellow bell pepper, thinly sliced
4 ounces / 112g pasture-raised boneless skinless chicken breasts or thighs, cut into ¼-inch strips
¼ teaspoon / 1g paprika
¼ teaspoon / 1g ground cumin
½ teaspoon / 2g ground coriander
¼ teaspoon / 3g Himalayan pink salt
pinch black pepper
1½ cups / 50g mixed baby greens
¼ cup / 44g Pico de Gallo (p. 81)
¼ cup Sweet Potato Hash (recipe from Breakfast Tacos, p. 71)
¼ cup / 62g Nacho Coconut Cheese (p. 221), warmed
½ a medium / 68g avocado, sliced
1 teaspoon / 1g chopped cilantro

TO MAKE THE CAULIFLOWER RICE:

1) Grate the cauliflower with a box grater or pulse in a food processor to a "rice like" consistency. Set aside.
2) In a large sauté pan, heat the avocado oil over medium flame. Add the onion and sauté until translucent. Add the garlic and continue sautéing for another minute. Add the riced cauliflower, salt and pepper, and stir to combine.
3) Add the vegetable stock, cover, and simmer for 5 minutes. Remove the lid and continue cooking until the cauliflower is dry.
4) Remove the pan from the heat and toss the "rice" with cilantro, lime zest, and lime juice.

TO MAKE THE BOWL:

1) In a sauté pan, heat 1 tablespoon of the avocado oil over medium flame. Add the onions and sauté until translucent. Add the garlic and continue cooking for 2 minutes. Add the peppers and cook until tender. Season with a pinch of salt and pepper, transfer the mixture to a bowl, and set aside.
2) Heat the remaining 1 tablespoon of avocado oil in the pan. Add the chicken pieces and season with paprika, cumin, coriander, salt, and pepper. Sauté until the chicken is browned and cooked through, about 10 minutes.
3) Place the mixed baby greens in a salad bowl and top with ½ cup of the caulifower rice, plus the chicken, peppers, pico de gallo, and sweet potato hash.
4) Drizzle with nacho cheese and garnish with avocado and cilantro.

BASIL & TOMATO PIZZA

MAKES ONE 8" PIZZA

One of the recipes that I served at my very first coconut dinner party, this has fooled many people who thought they were having the "real" thing! This is a classic margherita pizza with a twist–here we top our grain-free pizza base with melty coconut cheese, fresh basil, and heirloom tomatoes. If you've got pizza rounds in the freezer and coconut cheese on hand, this is a quick and easy option to throw together.

INGREDIENTS:
1 Pizza Base (p. 229)
1 recipe cherry tomato sauce from Yucca Croquettes (p. 110)
1 large or 2 small / 135g heirloom tomatoes, sliced into rounds
4-5 / 80g slices Coconut Cheese (p. 219)
pinch Himalayan pink salt
pinch black pepper
small handful / 4g of basil leaves

METHOD:
1) Preheat the oven to 425°F.
2) Spread the cherry tomato sauce onto the pizza round, making sure to leave a ¼-inch border around the edge. Arrange the tomato rounds and sliced coconut cheese on top. Sprinkle with salt and pepper.
3) Place the pizza on a sheet pan and pop in the oven for 10-15 minutes, until the cheese is bubbly and starts to brown slightly. Remove from the oven and garnish with basil leaves.
4) Cut into 6-8 wedges and serve immediately.

SPINACH CHEESE PIZZA

MAKES ONE 8" PIZZA

Our Spinach Cheese Dip makes a perfect topping in this easy, satisfying, plant-based pizza. Enjoy as it is, or load it with fresh greens, asparagus, avocado, and other seasonal veggies.

INGREDIENTS:

1 teaspoon / 4g avocado oil
1 cup / 70g sliced cremini mushrooms
pinch Himalayan pink salt
pinch black pepper
⅔ cup / 165g Spinach Cheese Dip (p. 87)
1 Pizza Base (p. 229)
microgreens, to garnish

METHOD:

1) Preheat the oven to 400°F.
2) Heat the avocado oil in a sauté pan over medium flame. Add the mushrooms and sauté until dry; season with salt and pepper.
3) Spread the spinach cheese dip over the pizza round, making sure to leave a ¼-inch border around the edge. Top with the sautéed mushrooms.
4) Place the pizza on a sheet pan and bake in the oven for 10-15 minutes, until the cheese is bubbly.
5) Cut into wedges and sprinkle with microgreens to serve.

BARBECUE PIZZA

MAKES ONE 8" PIZZA

This unique pizza, which gets its wonderfully smoky flavor from our clean BBQ Sauce, can be made with either chicken or jackfruit. In fact, jackfruit works so well with this sauce that it can be hard to differentiate between the two! I always suggest serving pizza—even grain-free—with a big salad on the side (or even right on top!). As with most of our dishes, avocado works really well as an additional topping here, too.

INGREDIENTS:

1 organic, pasture-raised chicken breast
or 2 chicken thighs
or 1 cup / 86g packed dried jackfruit
1 tablespoon / 14g avocado oil
pinch Himalayan pink salt
pinch black pepper
¼ medium / 37g red onion, thinly sliced
½ cup / 144g BBQ Sauce (p. 234)
¼ cup / 40g diced pineapple
1 Pizza Base (p. 229)
small handful cilantro leaves

METHOD:

1) Preheat the oven to 400°F.
2) Cut the chicken into ¼-inch strips.
3) Heat the avocado oil in a sauté pan over medium flame. Add the chicken pieces and sauté until browned and cooked through, about 5-8 minutes; season with salt and pepper. Transfer to a bowl and toss with the sliced red onion and ¼ cup of the BBQ sauce (if using jackfruit, simply sub in the dehydrated jackfruit for the cooked chicken here).
4) Spread the remaining BBQ sauce over the pizza round, making sure to leave a ¼-inch border around the edges; top with the chicken mixture and diced pineapple.
5) Place the pizza on a sheet pan and pop in the oven for 10-15 minutes.
6) Cut into 6-8 wedges and sprinkle with cilantro leaves to serve.

GREEN TOMATILLO ENCHILADAS

SERVES 2

Enchiladas Suizas (which translates to Swiss enchiladas) is a popular Mexican dish typically made with tomatillo sauce, lots of cheese, and some sort of cream or sour cream. It's incredibly delicious, but way too rich for me, so we developed this lighter, dairy-free version. You still get the tangy tomatillo sauce and the gooey cheesy texture, just not the tummy ache afterward! Just like the Mushroom & Tomato Enchiladas (page 145), these are a great thing to have in the freezer, so it's worth making multiple batches. Jackfruit or chicken works interchangeably as a filling in this recipe—just toss the jackfruit with a little of the tomatillo sauce before assembling the enchiladas.

FOR THE TOMATILLO SAUCE:
- 5 tomatillos, papery husks removed, cleaned, and halved
- ½ medium / 60g onion, roughly chopped
- 1 clove / 5g garlic, peeled
- 1 small / 5g jalapeño, seeded
- ½ bunch / 20g cilantro
- 2 tablespoons / 28g lime juice
- ¼ teaspoon / 3g Himalayan pink salt
- ¼ teaspoon / 1g black pepper

FOR THE ENCHILADAS:
- 1 tablespoon / 14g avocado oil
- ½ medium / 60g onion, thinly sliced
- 2 cloves / 10g garlic, minced
- 1½ pounds / 680g organic, pasture-raised, boneless, skinless chicken thighs or breasts, cut into strips
- ½ teaspoon / 1g ground coriander
- ¼ teaspoon / 3g Himalayan pink salt
- ¼ teaspoon / 1g black pepper
- 4 Coconut Flour Tortillas (p. 43) or store-bought
- 10 slices Coconut Cheese (p. 219)
- 1 tablespoon / 10g cilantro, chopped

TO MAKE THE TOMATILLO SAUCE:
1) Purée all ingredients in a blender; set aside.

TO MAKE THE ENCHILADAS:
1) Preheat the oven to 400°F.
2) In a large sauté pan, heat the avocado oil over medium flame. Add the onions and sauté until translucent. Add the garlic and saute for 1-2 minutes more. Add the chicken pieces, season with coriander, salt and pepper, and sauté until the chicken is cooked through; set aside.
3) Spoon a thin layer of the sauce into the bottom of an 8-inch cast iron skillet or oven-safe casserole dish.
4) Place 2 slices of coconut cheese on each tortilla, top with some of the chicken mixture, and roll so that the seam is facing down. Place them into the skillet or dish, side by side, spoon over the remaining sauce, and top with the remaining coconut cheese.
5) Bake for about 15-20 minutes, until the cheese has started to melt.
6) Garnish with chopped cilantro just before serving.

TIP: If you are planning to freeze these to use later, use a tempered glass oven- and freezer-safe dish and freeze after step 4. To cook, remove the lid of the dish, cover with a piece of parchment and bake for 40-45 minutes at 400°F until cooked through and the cheese is bubbling.

TIP: If you are planning to freeze these to use later, use a tempered glass, oven- and freezer-safe dish and freeze after step 4. To cook, remove the lid of the dish, cover with a piece of parchment and bake for 40-45 minutes at 400°F until cooked through and the cheese is bubbling.

MUSHROOM & TOMATO ENCHILADAS

SERVES 2

These enchiladas have all the deliciousness of a traditional recipe, but without the corn tortillas and cheese sauce to upset the tummy! And it's another great freezer meal. We recommend making multiple batches in one go and freezing in tempered glass dishes; that way, you can throw them straight into the oven for a quick and easy weeknight dinner. Serve with our Baby Kale Salad (page 95), Radish & Arugula Salad (page 93), or large handfuls of greens and avocado.

FOR THE ENCHILADA SAUCE:
1 tablespoon / 14g avocado oil
2 medium / 74g carrots, peeled and roughly chopped
2 stalks / 60g celery, roughly chopped
½ medium / 60g onion, roughly chopped
2 tablespoons / 36g tomato paste
1 medium / 8g jalapeño, seeded and roughly chopped
2 cloves / 10g garlic, roughly chopped
6 medium / 360g Roma tomatoes, roughly chopped
½ teaspoon / 4g Himalayan pink salt
¼ teaspoon / 1g black pepper
½ cup / 128g Coconut Milk (p. 215) or canned

FOR THE ENCHILADAS:
1 tablespoon / 14g avocado oil
½ medium / 60g onion, thinly sliced
2 cloves / 10g garlic, minced
1 cup / 70g cremini mushrooms, sliced
½ small / 225g acorn squash, peeled, seeds removed, and thinly sliced into half moons
1 medium / 180g zucchini, julienned
½ teaspoon / 4g Himalayan pink salt
¼ tsp. / 1g black pepper
4 Coconut Flour Tortillas (p. 43) or store-bought
10 slices Coconut Cheese (p. 219)
1 tablespoon / 3g cilantro, chopped

TO MAKE THE ENCHILADA SAUCE:
1) Heat the avocado oil in a medium saucepan. Add the carrot, celery and onion; sauté until the onions are translucent. Add the tomato paste and cook for 2-3 minutes. Add the jalapeño and garlic and cook for another 2-3 minutes. If the veggies begin to stick or burn, add up to ½ cup of water to loosen up any stuck-on bits at the bottom.
2) Add the Roma tomatoes, salt and pepper and bring the mixture up to a simmer. Cook for about 1 hour, until thickened.
3) Transfer the sauce to a blender, add the coconut milk, and purée until smooth. Season to taste with salt and pepper and set aside.

TO MAKE THE ENCHILADAS:
1) Preheat the oven to 400°F.
2) Heat the avocado oil in a large sauté pan. Add the onions and sauté until translucent. Add garlic and sauté for 1-2 minutes. Add the cremini mushrooms and cook until dry, about 5-7 minutes. Add the acorn squash and zucchini, season with salt and pepper, and sauté until the squash is tender.
3) Spoon a thin layer of the sauce into the bottom of an 8-inch cast iron skillet or oven-safe casserole dish.
4) Place 2 slices of coconut cheese on each tortilla, top with some of the veggie mixture, and roll so that the seam is facing down. Place them into the skillet or dish, side by side, spoon over the remaining sauce, and top with the remaining coconut cheese.
5) Bake for about 15-20 minutes, until the cheese has started to melt.
6) Garnish with chopped cilantro just before serving.

VEGGIE BURGER

MAKES 6 PATTIES

Most veggie burgers rely heavily on beans or legumes, which can, unfortunately, be tough for some people to digest. Ours, on the other hand, have a base of plantain and sweet potato, with an added protein boost from hemp and pumpkin seeds. The liquid smoke lends a hint of smoky flavor, but these are even better grilled on the barbecue. My favorite way to serve these burgers is wrapped in butter lettuce and loaded with grilled red onions, avocado, Dijon mustard and BBQ Sauce (page 234), or in a deconstructed burger bowl layered onto salad and drizzled with Chipotle Coconut Cheese (page 220). Yum!

INGREDIENTS:

3 cups / 300g grated sweet potato
2 cups / 200g grated green plantains
3 tablespoons / 20g ground chia seeds
3 ounces / 100g water
2½ tablespoons / 40g Hemp Tahini (p. 222)
2 tablespoons / 20g vegetable soup base powder (we like Seitenbacher brand)
1 teaspoon / 5g liquid smoke
⅓ cup / 40g ground pumpkin seeds
1 cup / 156g frozen spinach, thawed and any excess liquid squeezed out
1 teaspoon / 8g Himalayan pink salt
½ teaspoon / 3g black pepper

METHOD:

1) Preheat the oven to 350°F.
2) Spread out the grated sweet potato and plantain on two sheet pans lined with parchment paper. Pop in the oven and bake for 20 minutes, just to dry out slightly.
3) In a medium mixing bowl, stir together the ground chia seeds and water; allow to sit for 5 minutes. Add the hemp tahini, vegetable soup powder, and liquid smoke; stir well to combine.
4) Add the sweet potato, plantains, pumpkin seeds, spinach, salt and pepper and use your hands to mix well; divide into 6 patties.
5) Place on a sheet pan lined with parchment paper and bake for 30 minutes. Flip the patties over and bake for an additional 10-15 minutes.

Serve with Yucca Fries and Ketchup.
Pages 116 & 233

LIFLOWER NACHO CHEESE

2

I loved cauliflower cheese (a popular English dish made with loads of butter, milk, and cheese) when I was growing up, so ever since I stopped eating dairy, I've wanted to figure out a "cleaned-up" version. The answer is nacho coconut cheese! This lighter, vegan twist pays homage to my childhood favorite, but never leaves me feeling weighed down or uncomfortable. Serve this as a main dish on a bed of greens or vegetables, or as a side with simply cooked protein.

INGREDIENTS:

1 head cauliflower, cut into florets
2 tablespoons / 28g avocado oil
¼ teaspoon / 3g Himalayan pink salt
¼ teaspoon / 1g black pepper
1 cup / 280g Nacho Coconut Cheese (p. 221)

METHOD:

1) Preheat the oven to 425°F.
2) Toss the cauliflower with avocado oil, salt and pepper to coat. Spread onto a sheet pan lined with parchment paper or a silicone mat and bake for about 10 minutes, until browned.
3) Transfer the cooked cauliflower to an oven-safe casserole dish. Pour nacho cheese over the top and bake for 5-10 minutes, until the cheese is bubbly.

SWEET TREATS

The grab & go counter at the Real Coconut is where you'll find many of our sweet treats—perfect for a post-yoga snack, or to take home to savor later. It has become a bit of a destination in its own right, so it's wonderful to be able to share some of our customers' favorite recipes in this section. As you can imagine, baking without grains is a real science—without gluten or grains (or even the pseudo-grains we also avoid) to help bind things together, you really have to get creative. Developing these recipes required a good amount of trial and error, but once you've got your grain-free pantry stocked, actually making them is very easy!

We try to keep as many of these sweets as possible fully inclusive (i.e., no eggs and no nuts); however, some recipes just can't work without one or the other, so if you're sensitive to either or both, be sure to reference the key at the top of each recipe. Thankfully, we've got a really robust selection here, so no matter your tastes or dietary restrictions, you are certain to find something to satisfy your sweet tooth.

APPLE CIDER DONUTS

MAKES 6 MEDIUM DONUTS

My English friends will berate me for spelling these the American way (we write doughnuts), but whichever way you write it, these donuts taste ridiculously amazing, so hopefully all will be forgiven! The apple cider and spices combination gives a bit of a holiday vibe, but I love these any time of year. The glaze can be omitted to lower the sweetness, but it's so good that I would suggest a small drizzle at the least. These are super impressive to serve to guests, and if you want to make your mixture go further, invest in mini donut molds for cute little versions!

FOR THE DONUTS:

¾ cup / 180g apple cider
½ cup / 100g coconut sugar
⅓ cup + 4 teaspoons / 58g blanched superfine almond flour
½ cup / 58g tapioca flour
½ cup / 48g coconut flour
1½ teaspoon / 7g baking soda
1½ teaspoon / 7g baking powder
pinch Himalayan pink salt
1 teaspoon / 3g cinnamon
1 teaspoon / 3g vanilla extract
¾ teaspoon / 2g ground nutmeg
¼ teaspoon / 1g ground cloves
4 tablespoons / 60g coconut oil, melted
⅓ cup / 68g unsweetened applesauce, room temperature
1½ teaspoons / 8g apple cider vinegar

FOR THE GLAZE:

1 cup / 120g fine maple sugar (or 200g turbinado sugar)
2-4 tablespoons / 30-60g apple cider

METHOD:

1) Place the apple cider in a small saucepan over medium-low flame and cook until reduced by half. Set aside.
2) Preheat oven to 350°F.
3) Combine the dry ingredients in a medium bowl; whisk to blend.
4) In a separate bowl, whisk together the reduced apple cider, coconut oil, applesauce and apple cider vinegar. Pour the wet ingredients into the dry and stir to combine.
5) Pour the batter into a piping bag and pipe into silicone donut molds.
6) Pop in the oven and bake for 25-30 minutes; set aside to cool.
7) To make the glaze, stir together the sugar and apple cider until very smooth; dip (or drizzle over) the donuts.

BUTTERMILK DONUTS

MAKES 7 MEDIUM DONUTS

These buttermilk donuts have a wonderfully subtle flavor, just a hint of vanilla and a slight tang from the buttermilk–and pairs beautifully with the maple/coconut glaze. The buttermilk needs to sit overnight in the fridge, so be sure to plan ahead. That being said, if you're desperate for donuts NOW, you can always replace it with a dairy-free milk of your choice.

FOR THE COCONUT BUTTERMILK:
½ cup / 120g Coconut Milk (p. 215) or canned
½ tablespoon / 7g lemon juice
½ tablespoon / 7g apple cider vinegar

FOR THE DONUTS:
4 tablespoons / 56g coconut oil, melted
⅓ cup / 68g unsweetened applesauce, room temperature
1½ teaspoons / 8g apple cider vinegar
½ cup / 48g coconut sugar
⅓ cup + 4 teaspoons / 58g blanched superfine almond flour
½ cup / 58g tapioca flour
5½ tablespoons / 48g coconut flour
1½ teaspoons / 7g baking soda
1½ teaspoons / 7g baking powder
pinch Himalayan pink salt

FOR THE GLAZE:
1 cup / 120g fine maple sugar (or 200g turbinado sugar)
2-4 tablespoons / 30-60g Coconut Milk (p. 215) or canned

TO MAKE THE COCONUT BUTTERMILK:
1) Whisk together coconut buttermilk ingredients and refrigerate overnight.

TO MAKE THE DONUTS:
1) Preheat oven to 325°F.
2) Melt the coconut oil in large bowl set over a pot of simmering water. Remove from the heat and whisk in the apple cider vinegar, coconut sugar and buttermilk. Add the remaining ingredients and whisk to combine.
3) Transfer the batter to a piping bag and pipe into greased silicone donut molds.
4) Pop in the oven and bake for 30 minutes; set aside to cool.
5) To make the glaze, add coconut milk to maple sugar a little at a time, stirring constantly, until a glaze consistency is achieved.
6) Drizzle the glaze over the donuts and allow it to harden before serving.

BANANA BREAD

MAKES ONE 9" LOAF   E

A classic favorite, and the perfect way to use up overripe bananas (the ripeness does make a difference to the consistency and sweetness). In my opinion, the chocolate chips are a worthwhile indulgence here, but you can certainly omit them for a lighter option. I always slice and freeze any leftovers; that way I can pull out slices as needed, defrost, then crisp up in a pan for a quick breakfast or afternoon treat.

INGREDIENTS:

2 cups + 1 tablespoon / 210g blanched superfine almond flour

½ cup / 55g tapioca flour

1¾ teaspoon / 8g baking soda

¾ teaspoon / 3g aluminum-free baking powder

pinch Himalayan pink salt

4 eggs, room temperature

1 teaspoon / 3g vanilla extract

¼ cup / 54g coconut oil, melted

3 tablespoons / 40g coconut sugar

3 medium / 350g bananas, very ripe, mashed well

¾ cup / 160g dairy-free semi-sweet chocolate chips

METHOD:

1) Preheat oven to 325°F.

2) In a medium bowl, whisk together the almond flour, tapioca flour, baking soda, baking powder, and salt.

3) In another bowl, whisk together the eggs, vanilla, coconut oil, and coconut sugar. Add the mashed bananas and stir to combine.

4) Stir in the dry ingredients, then fold in the chocolate chips.

5) Transfer the batter to a greased 9.25" x 5.25" loaf pan lined with parchment paper. Bake for about 1 hour, or until a toothpick comes out clean. Cool completely before serving.

CHOCOLATE CHIP COOKIES

MAKES 16 SMALL COOKIES

After our plantain bread recipe, these cookies were the next stage in our plantain revolution! We put these in the rooms at Sanará Tulum for our guests and serve mini versions with the checks at the restaurant. We knew we were onto a winner when people kept coming back for more, and asking to buy huge bags of them to take home! A quick and easy cookie recipe (not to mention grain- and egg-free!), this will surely become a new go-to favorite.

INGREDIENTS:

4 teaspoons / 10g ground chia seeds

¼ cup / 50g water

4 tablespoons / 70g Almond Butter (p. 223) or store-bought

3 tablespoons / 42g coconut oil

½ cup / 115g coconut sugar

1 cup / 125g plantain flour

½ teaspoon / 4g baking soda

pinch Himalayan pink salt

½ cup / 80g dairy-free chocolate chips

METHOD:

1) Preheat oven to 350°F.
2) Stir together the ground chia seeds and water; let sit for 5 minutes to make a "chia egg."
3) In a stand mixer, beat together the almond butter, coconut oil, and coconut sugar until well combined. Mix in the chia egg.
4) In a small bowl, whisk together the plantain flour, baking soda, and salt. Add to wet ingredients and mix well. Stir in the chocolate chips.
5) Scoop the dough into golf ball size pieces and press down to form a disc.
6) Place on a sheet pan lined with parchment paper and bake for 14-16 minutes.
7) Remove from the oven and let cool. Cookies can be stored in an airtight container at room temperature for up to 2 weeks.

GINGER SNAP COOKIES

MAKES 24 COOKIES

Ginger Snaps have always been a favorite of mine, but the usual, commercially bought options and traditional recipes don't work with my digestion. Our version, which uses plantain flour as a base, is such a welcome treat that I can actually enjoy! Use gingerbread-man cutters to transform these into festive cookies for the Holidays.

INGREDIENTS:

4 teaspoons / 10g ground chia seeds
¼ cup / 50g water
4 tablespoons / 70g Almond Butter (p. 223) or store-bought
3 tablespoons / 42g coconut oil
½ cup / 100g coconut sugar
1 tablespoon / 15g molasses
1 cup / 130g plantain flour
½ teaspoon / 3g baking soda
1½ teaspoon / 4g ground ginger
½ teaspoon / 2g ground cinnamon
¼ teaspoon / pinch ground nutmeg
¼ teaspoon / pinch ground allspice
pinch Himalayan pink salt

METHOD:

1) Preheat oven to 250°F.
2) Stir together the ground chia seeds and water; let sit for 5 minutes to make a "chia egg."
3) In a stand mixer, beat the almond butter, coconut oil, coconut sugar and molasses until well combined. Mix in the chia egg.
4) In a small bowl, combine the plantain flour, baking soda, ground ginger, cinnamon, nutmeg, allspice and salt. Add the wet ingredients and beat until smooth.
5) Form the dough into a flat disc. Wrap and chill in fridge for about 1 hour, or until firm.
6) Roll the chilled dough to ¼-inch thickness; chill again if the dough becomes too soft. Cut into circles with a 2-inch ring mold (unused dough can be pressed together, rechilled, rolled and cut).
7) Transfer the cookies to a sheet pan lined with parchment paper and bake in the oven for 1 hour 20 minutes.
8) Cool completely before serving. You can store these in an airtight container at room temperature for several weeks.

HEMP RAISIN COOKIES

MAKES 16 SMALL COOKIES   **E**

The third option in our plantain flour cookie trilogy adds hemp seeds and raisins, creating a twist on an oatmeal raisin cookie with the benefit of added protein! People usually have a favorite out of the three, but I love them all too much to choose one!

INGREDIENTS:

4 teaspoon / 10g ground chia seeds

¼ cup / 50g water

4 tablespoons / 70g Almond Butter (p. 223) or store-bought

3 tablespoons / 42g coconut oil

½ cup / 115g coconut sugar

1 cup / 125g plantain flour

½ teaspoon / 4g baking soda

¾ teaspoon / 2g ground cinnamon

⅓ cup / 70g hemp seeds

pinch Himalayan pink salt

¾ cup / 110g raisins

METHOD:

1) Preheat the oven to 350°F.
2) Stir together the ground chia seeds and water; let sit for 5 minutes to make a "chia egg."
3) In a stand mixer, beat together the almond butter, coconut oil and coconut sugar until well combined. Mix in the chia egg.
4) In a small bowl, whisk together the plantain flour, baking soda, cinnamon, hemp seeds and salt. Stir into the wet ingredients and mix well. Stir in the raisins.
5) Scoop the dough into golf ball size pieces and press down to form a disc.
6) Place on a sheet pan lined with parchment paper and bake for 14-16 minutes.
7) Remove from the oven and let cool. Cookies can be stored in an airtight container at room temperature for up to 2 weeks.

RAISIN SCONES

MAKES 8 SCONES

Better than any coffee shop scones, these are just the right amount of dense and just the right amount of sweet (and being English, I have strong opinions about scones!). These are a wonderful accompaniment for morning or afternoon tea, served on their own or with jam and Coconut Whipped Cream (page 238) for an extra special ritual/indulgence. You can also mix up the fruit, depending on what's in season, and add in what you're craving–blueberries work well, as do chocolate chips for a cheeky chocolatey version!!

INGREDIENTS:

1 cup / 100g blanched superfine almond flour
½ cup / 60g tapioca flour
¾ cup / 80g coconut flour
1 teaspoon / 2g psyllium husk flakes
¼ cup / 50g coconut sugar
1½ teaspoons / 12g baking powder
pinch Himalayan pink salt
¼ cup / 55g cold coconut oil
1 cup / 225g Coconut Milk (p. 215) or canned
1 cup / 135g raisins
turbinado sugar, for sprinkling on top

METHOD:

1) Whisk together almond flour, tapioca flour, coconut flour, psyllium husk, coconut sugar, baking powder, and salt. Using your hands (don't use a machine for this!), mix in coconut oil until well incorporated and you achieve a crumbly texture.

2) Add the coconut milk and continue mixing with your hands to form a dough. Add the raisins and mix to combine.

3) Form the dough into a disc (approx 1" x 7-8") and chill in the fridge for at least 1 hour.

4) When ready to bake, preheat the oven to 325°F.

5) Remove the dough from fridge and cut into 8 triangles. Place the triangles on a parchment-lined sheet pan, leaving at least a 1-inch space between each. Sprinkle the scones with turbinado sugar and bake for 45-50 minutes.

6) Serve warm with your favorite jam!

CINNAMON ROLLS

SERVES 8

These cinnamon rolls are unbelievably good and have converted many a grain-free, dairy-free dessert skeptic! They're a bit of work to make at home, but so worth the effort for a special occasion, a lazy weekend, or to impress guests. Look for butter-flavored coconut oil in the coconut oil section at grocery stores or order online; we like Nutiva brand.

FOR THE DOUGH:

1 cup / 236g + 1 / 15g tablespoon Coconut Milk (p. 215) or canned

1½ tablespoons / 30g + 2½ / 50g tablespoons maple syrup

2½ teaspoons / 10g yeast

1¼ cups / 145g blanched superfine almond flour

¾ cup + 4 teaspoons / 100g tapioca flour

⅔ cup / 75g coconut flour

pinch Himalayan pink salt

2 teaspoons / 10g baking powder

2 teaspoons / 4g psyllium husk flakes

4 tablespoons / 55g butter-flavored coconut oil

FOR THE FILLING:

¾ cup / 150g coconut sugar

½ cup / 132g butter-flavored coconut oil

2 tablespoons / 28g ground cinnamon

FOR THE GLAZE:

½ cup / 100g turbinado sugar

1 tablespoon / 10g ground cinnamon

1-2 tablespoons / 15-30g Coconut Milk (p. 215) or canned

METHOD:

1) Preheat oven to 325°F.
2) Heat the coconut milk to about 100°F. In a small bowl, stir together the 1½ tablespoons maple syrup, yeast and warm coconut milk; cover and set aside until foamy.
3) In another bowl, stir together dry ingredients; set aside.
4) In the bowl of a stand mixer, combine the butter-flavored coconut oil, remaining 2½ tablespoons maple syrup and yeast mixture. Stir with paddle attachment just to combine. Add dry ingredients and beat until well combined (about 5 minutes).
5) Transfer to a greased bowl, cover with a clean towel, and set aside to proof for 1 hour.
6) Meanwhile, stir together the filling ingredients until well combined.
7) Dust a sheet of parchment paper and the dough with extra tapioca flour to prevent sticking. Roll out dough to a 10" x 13" rectangle.
8) Spread an even layer of filling over the dough, leaving a 1-inch border.
9) Starting from shorter edge and using the parchment as a guide, roll the dough into a log. Cut the log into 8 pieces and place, cut side up, into a greased pie dish.
10) Cover with a clean towel and let rise for another 30 minutes.
11) Remove the towel and cover loosely with foil. Bake for 30 minutes; remove foil and continue baking, uncovered, for another 30 minutes.
12) To make the glaze, blend the turbinado sugar to a fine powder in a NutriBullet. Transfer to a small bowl and stir in the cinnamon. Add the coconut milk, 1 teaspoon at a time, until a glaze-like texture is achieved.
13) Drizzle over warm cinnamon rolls and serve immediately.

BROWNIES

MAKES 8 BROWNIES

The fudgiest of brownies, and no grains, eggs or refined sugar here! I don't know if it's even possible to describe the yumminess in words . . . so the only way you will know is if you make them! These brownies go fast, so I recommend making a double batch, just in case you have to share.

INGREDIENTS:

2 teaspoons / 5g ground chia seeds
5 teaspoons / 25g water
4 tablespoons / 56g avocado oil + extra for greasing the pan
¼ cup / 52g coconut oil, melted
¾ cup / 250g maple syrup
2 teaspoons / 8g vanilla extract
⅓ cup / 40g cassava flour
¼ cup / 30g coconut flour
4 tablespoons / 30g cacao powder
¼ teaspoon / 1g baking soda
pinch Himalayan pink salt

METHOD:

1) Preheat oven to 325°F.
2) Brush a 9.25"x 5.25" loaf pan with avocado oil, line with parchment paper, and brush with a little more avocado oil.
3) Stir together the ground chia seeds and water; let sit for 5 minutes to make a "chia egg."
4) In a large bowl, whisk together the avocado oil, coconut oil, maple syrup and vanilla extract. Add the chia egg and whisk to combine.
5) In a separate bowl, stir together the cassava flour, coconut flour, cacao powder, baking soda, and salt.
6) Add the dry ingredients to the wet ingredients and whisk to combine.
7) Pour the batter into the prepared loaf pan and tap on the counter to remove any air bubbles.
8) Bake for 30-35 minutes, until the top is set and dry and the inside is still slightly wet. Cool completely before cutting into 8 squares. These can be stored in an airtight container in the fridge for up to one week.

BLUEBERRY YOGURT FROZEN POPS

MAKES 6 POPSICLES

This recipe has such easy components, but if you're going for the full visual effect (which looks incredible and requires adding layers every hour or so), choose a day when you're hanging around the house. The cheat's version, which tastes the same and still looks quite impressive, is to swirl the mixtures together in the mold. If you like your popsicles a little sweeter, just add a splash of maple syrup in with the blueberry mix. Feel free to play around with different fruits; raspberries, strawberries, and mangos are all options I love.

INGREDIENTS:

1 cup / 235g Coconut Yogurt (p. 49) or store-bought

1 cup / 140g frozen blueberries

METHOD:

1) In a blender or food processor, roughly purée half of the coconut yogurt with the frozen blueberries (you don't want it completely smooth).

2) Spoon about 2 tablespoons of the blueberry mixture into the well of each popsicle mold. Tap lightly to knock out any air bubbles; freeze for 1 hour.

3) Remove the molds from freezer, and spoon about 2 tablespoons of the plain coconut yogurt into each well. Tap lightly and freeze for another hour.

4) Repeat steps 2 and 3 until the popsicle molds are full. Press popsicle sticks firmly into each well and freeze until fully set (at least 4 hours).

5) To unmold, briefly dip the mold into warm water, and gently pull on the sticks.

DULCE DE LECHE TRUFFLES

MAKES 16 TRUFFLES

I love a little bit of chocolate with a cup of fresh mint tea in the evening, and one of these truffles does the trick for me! If you like a firmer caramel center, pull these out of the fridge just before eating; or for a more gooey experience, leave them out at room temperature for half an hour. Either way, the coconut dulce de leche filling is divine!

INGREDIENTS:
1 recipe dulce de leche, chilled (from Stewed Apple and Dulce de Leche Quesadilla, p. 175),
8 ounces / 225g dairy-free semi-sweet chocolate

METHOD:
1) Using a teaspoon, scoop out the chilled dulce de leche and quickly roll into 16 balls. Place them on a sheet pan and pop in the freezer for 1 hour.
2) Meanwhile, melt the chocolate over a double boiler, stirring until smooth; cool to room temperature.
3) Working quickly, drop each ball of dulce de leche into the chocolate and coat completely (if the dulce de leche is softening too quickly, you can pop the balls back into the freezer to firm them up).
4) Remove the truffles with a fork, return them to the sheet pan, and return to the freezer for 30 minutes.
5) Store in an airtight container in the fridge for several weeks.

GINGER CAKE

MAKES ONE 9" LOAF

This cake is reminiscent of an old favorite packaged cake that can be found in England, called Jamaica Ginger Cake (the name stems from its original Jamaican roots). The mineral-dense molasses gives this cake its deep, rich flavor, which marries perfectly with the slightly spicy ginger. We use fresh plantain—with only the tiniest amount of plantain flour—combined with eggs, to make this cake deliciously moist. It certainly tastes like a treat, but with no added sugar, this is actually something you can enjoy for breakfast or any time of the day. It also packs up well and makes an excellent plane snack when I'm traveling!

INGREDIENTS:

2 eggs
2 medium-size / 150g ripe plantains, peeled
1 teaspoon / 4g vanilla extract
⅓ cup / 55g molasses
3 tablespoons / 40g coconut oil
1 tablespoon / 20g fresh ginger, grated
2 tablespoons / 15g plantain flour
3½ teaspoons / 9g ground ginger
¾ teaspoon / 2g ground cinnamon
¾ teaspoon / 2g ground nutmeg
½ teaspoon / 2g ground allspice
¾ teaspoon / 3g baking soda

METHOD:

1) Preheat the oven to 350°F.
2) In a blender, combine the eggs, plantain, vanilla extract, molasses, coconut oil and grated ginger; blend until smooth.
3) In a small bowl, whisk together the plantain flour, ground ginger, cinnamon, nutmeg, allspice and baking soda. Add to the blender with the wet ingredients and blend until smooth.
4) Grease a 9.25" x 5.25" loaf pan and line with parchment paper. Pour batter into pan and bake for about 1 hour, or until a skewer inserted in the center comes out clean.
5) Cool to room temperature before slicing. Cake can be stored in an airtight container at room temperature for 2-3 days or in the fridge for up to 1 week.

MACHO CACAO CAKE

MAKES ONE 9" LOAF

Just like our Macho Pancakes (page 57), this recipe gets its name from the key ingredient, plantains, which are known in Mexico as platano macho. Using fresh, ripe plantains keeps this cake unbelievably moist and light. I've been eating it for years, and never tire of it! It also makes a perfect birthday cake when baked in a round mold, covered with extra chocolate ganache and drizzled with the coulis—I've served it countless times, and it never fails to impress!

FOR THE GANACHE:

1 cup / 250g Coconut Milk (p. 215) or canned
1 cup / 150g dairy-free, bittersweet chocolate or chocolate chips, 74%

FOR THE CAKE:

5 eggs
2 medium / 150g ripe plantains, peeled
1½ medium / 180g bananas, very ripe
¼ cup / 55g coconut oil
¼ cup / 70g maple syrup + 1 tablespoon / 20g maple syrup
1 teaspoon / 2g vanilla extract
⅓ cup / 40g plantain flour
5 tablespoons / 40g cacao powder
1 teaspoon / 5g baking soda
1¼ cups / 200g semi-sweet chocolate chips

TO SERVE:

Coconut Whipped Cream (p. 238)
⅓ cup / 70g Raspberry Coulis (p. 238)
berries to garnish

TO MAKE THE GANACHE:

1) Heat the coconut milk in a small saucepan over medium flame. Bring it up to a low simmer, then remove from the heat and stir in the chocolate. Continue stirring until the chocolate is melted and smooth.
2) Allow to cool to room temperature before spreading onto the cake.

TO MAKE THE CAKE:

1) Preheat the oven to 350°F.
2) Purée the eggs, plantains, banana, coconut oil, ¼ cup maple syrup, and vanilla extract in a blender. Add the plantain flour, cacao powder and baking soda; continue blending until smooth.
3) Grease a 9.25" x 5.25" loaf pan and line with parchment paper. Pour the batter into the pan and stir in the chocolate chips.
4) Bake at 350°F for 35-40 minutes, or until a toothpick inserted into the center comes out clean. Remove the cake from the oven and allow to cool completely.

MACHO CACAO 8" LAYER CAKE

TO SERVE:
1) Unmold the cake from the loaf pan and cut into 2 layers.
2) Spoon a small amount of ganache onto the bottom slice and cover with the top layer. Spread ganache on the top of the cake.
3) Slice and serve with a dollop of coconut whipped cream, a drizzle of raspberry coulis, and fresh berries.

TO MAKE AN 8" LAYER CAKE:
1) Double the cake recipe.
2) If you want a very decadent cake, make 1.5 x the ganache recipe to cover completely.
3) Grease two 8" cake pans and line with parchment paper. Divide the batter evenly between each and stir in the chocolate chips.
4) Bake for 35-40 minutes, or until a toothpick inserted into the center comes out clean. Remove the cake from the oven and allow to cool completely.
5) Refrigerate the ganache until it's firm enough to spread like a frosting (about 30 minutes).
6) Unmold the cakes from the pans and spread a thin layer of ganache onto the top of one cake, and cover with the other. Using the remaining ganache, frost the top and sides of the cake.
7) Drizzle the coulis over the top.

SMOOTHIES, HYDRATION & WARM DRINKS

This book wouldn't be complete without the recipes for our beloved "ice cream" smoothies (which have become a bit of a phenomenon in Tulum, with people waiting up to an hour to get one during high season!) and some of the top favorites on our "Healthful Hydration" menu, as well as a few of our most popular blended coffees and warm drinks. From the beginning, I've made a point of keeping our drinks menu simple and honest, relying on the quality of the ingredients rather than showy techniques or a long list of supposed "superfood" add-ons. Fans of our smoothies may be surprised to learn that most are made with just five ingredients (many of which you'll likely already have in your freezer and pantry!), or that all of our frothy coffee concoctions can easily be whipped up in any home blender.

In Tulum, our coconut milk and almond butter are made from scratch (imagine how many coconuts need to be opened, the meat extracted, then the blending & squeezing for all the coconut milk we go through!), and the other ingredients are of the highest quality: the squidgiest, freshest Medjool dates from Mexicali, fresh local vanilla pods, and roasted Mexican cacao powder, along with gorgeously ripe bananas and mangos, frozen at the perfect moment.

Since most home cooks are not cracking open mature coconuts (if you'd like to, you can check out How to Open a Coconut, on page 37) or picking fresh mangos from nearby trees, you can easily prepare these drinks at home with fresh or canned coconut milk (or homemade almond milk, if you don't have coconut milk on hand), unroasted almond butter (with no added ingredients), organic frozen fruit, and the best-quality Medjool dates, cacao powder, and coffee beans you can source. Then sit back and dream of being at the beach!

VANILLA ALMOND BLISS

SERVES 1

I have to admit that I was addicted to this smoothie for a couple of years . . . I had to get my daily fix! Many vanilla lovers have now informed me that they, too, are addicts—my apologies for that! These days, the Choco Nutty (page 186) is my go-to, but this recipe, with its creamy texture and sweet vanilla flavor, will always have a special place in my heart.

INGREDIENTS:

4-5 / 60g Medjool dates, pitted

2 tablespoons / 45g unroasted Almond Butter (p. 223) or store-bought

½ teaspoon / 1g vanilla powder ¼ / 2g of a vanilla bean

¾ cup / 150g Coconut Milk (p. 215) or canned

1 cup / 220g ice

METHOD:

1) Purée the dates, almond butter, vanilla powder and coconut milk in a blender until smooth.
2) Add ice and blend until there are no more ice chunks.
3) Serve immediately.

TIP: Buy a big batch of bananas and ripen until they have lots of black spots. Peel, break into pieces, and freeze, to make the perfect "ice cream" smoothies.

'CO NUTTY

This is my top favorite smoothie of all time! Almost every time I go to either order or make a smoothie, I think about diversifying a bit with another choice, but somehow my Choco Nutty just calls out for me, and I can't resist! For an extra special treat, divide the smoothie into 2 smaller pots and pop in the freezer for 30 minutes to 1 hour, then enjoy with a spoon like ice cream (either share it, or keep one for later)!

INGREDIENTS:

3-4 / 45g Medjool dates, pitted
2 tablespoons / 30g unroasted Almond Butter (p. 223) or store-bought
½ teaspoon / 1g vanilla powder or ¼ / 2g of a vanilla bean
2 tablespoons / 15g cacao powder
½ cup / 150g Coconut Milk (p. 215) or canned
1 medium / 100g frozen banana
¾ cup / 200g ice

METHOD:

1) Purée the dates, almond butter, vanilla powder, cacao and coconut milk in a blender until smooth.
2) Add frozen banana and ice and blend until there are no more ice chunks.
3) Serve immediately.

MINT CHOC

SERVES 1

If you love mint and chocolate, you'll go crazy for this combination! A blissful marriage of the two, this refreshing, chocolatey treat tastes just like a mint chocolate chip milkshake, but is a whole lot better for you.

INGREDIENTS:

3-4 / 45g Medjool dates, pitted
½ cup / 150g Coconut Milk (p. 215) or canned
2 tablespoons / 15g cacao powder
¼ cup / 5g packed mint leaves
1 medium / 100g frozen banana
¾ cup / 200g ice

METHOD:

1) Puree the dates, coconut milk, cacao powder and mint leaves in a blender until smooth.
2) Add frozen banana and ice and blend until there are no ice chunks left.
3) Serve immediately.

BANANA SPLIT

SERVES 1

Our version of a traditional banana split, but with none of the preservatives, dairy, or refined sugar! It is definitely an indulgence (hello, chocolate chips!), so I usually reserve it for special occasions. As with all of our smoothies, we blend in a particular order so the end result is almost like ice cream. Be sure to follow the directions and enjoy immediately after blending!

INGREDIENTS:

3-4 / 50g Medjool dates, pitted

2 tablespoons / 30g unroasted Almond Butter (p. 223) or store-bought

¾ cup / 150g Coconut Milk (p215) or canned

½ teaspoon / 1g vanilla powder or ¼ of / 2g vanilla bean

1 medium / 100g frozen banana

¾ cup / 200g ice

1 heaping tablespoon / 20g dairy-free semi-sweet chocolate chips

METHOD:

1) Purée the dates, almond butter, coconut milk and vanilla powder in a blender until smooth.
2) Add frozen banana and ice and blend until there are no ice chunks left.
3) Add chocolate chips and blend for a few seconds, allowing the chips to break into tiny pieces and distribute throughout.
4) Serve immediately.

STRAWBERRIES & CREAM

When it comes to our smoothies, people usually have a go-to favorite, and it's fun to try to work out personalities based on preferences! From my ad hoc research, I find that they usually fall into one of three categories: chocoholics, smooth vanilla fans, or berry-licious lovers! This one is for the berry lovers out there. I always forget how much I love this smoothie when I have it because I'm usually too busy drinking my Choco Nutty (page 186)! This recipe has also converted many a child who came to the restaurant expecting to find a dairy milkshake.

INGREDIENTS:

3-4 / 50g Medjool dates, pitted
½ teaspoon / 1g vanilla powder or ¼ / 2g of a vanilla bean
1 cup / 200g Coconut Milk (p. 215) or canned
½ cup / 120g frozen strawberries
½ medium / 50g frozen banana
½ cup / 120g ice

METHOD:

1) Purée the dates, vanilla powder and coconut milk in a blender until smooth.
2) Add frozen strawberries, frozen banana and ice and blend until there are no more ice chunks.
3) Serve immediately.

COCOCCINO

SERVES 1

What happens when you take a Vanilla Almond Bliss (page 185) and add coffee to it? It becomes one of the world's best and cleanest Cino recipes! Loved by coffee aficionados since we opened, this recipe can easily be replicated at home. Make sure both the coffee and coconut milk are cold before you start, and keep your ice as solidly frozen as possible to get the most "ice creamy" version possible.

INGREDIENTS:

¼ cup / 56g coffee/espresso, cold

4-5 / 60g Medjool dates, pitted

2 tablespoons / 45g unroasted Almond Butter (p. 223) or store-bought

½ teaspoon / 1g vanilla powder or ¼ / 2g of a vanilla bean

¾ cup / 150g Coconut Milk (p. 215) or canned

1 cup / 220g ice

METHOD:

1) Purée the coffee, dates, almond butter, vanilla powder and coconut milk in a blender until smooth.
2) Add ice and blend until there are no more ice chunks.
3) Serve immediately.

MELON MINT COOLER

SERVES 1

This recipe was birthed during a sudden heat wave in the UK, when the idea of moving back to Mexico wasn't even in my mind. It was so hot that all I wanted was something ultra-refreshing and cooling to sip on, and this smoothie really hit the spot. With the generous amount of mint added, this becomes a real green smoothie! Using frozen melon makes it extra cool, and easy to make year-round; just be sure to stock up on, cut up, and freeze honeydew melons when they're in season, so you can make this any time the weather warms up. Enjoy this immediately, as it separates fairly quickly.

INGREDIENTS:

1 cup / 150g diced honeydew melon, cut up and frozen
1 cup / 150g green grapes
1 cup / 20g fresh mint leaves
2 tablespoons / 50g lime juice
½ cup / 120g ice

METHOD:

1) Purée the melon, grapes, mint and lime juice in a blender until smooth.
2) Add ice and blend until there are no more ice chunks.
3) Serve immediately.

MANGO LASSI

SERVES 1

Indian lassis usually rely on full-fat dairy yogurt as their base. Here, we replace this with coconut yogurt, which provides an easy to digest probiotic boost and a slight tartness to offset the sweetness of the mango and pineapple. At the restaurant, we cut up and freeze fresh pineapple and mango, but store-bought frozen fruit works well, too. You can play with the levels of yogurt for this fruity and refreshing drink, adding more or less as you please.

INGREDIENTS:

1 cup / 165g frozen mango chunks
¼ cup / 45g frozen pineapple chunks
½ cup / 110g Coconut Milk (p. 215) or canned
¼ cup / 60g Coconut Yogurt (p. 49) or store-bought
½ cup / 100g ice

METHOD:

1) Purée mango, pineapple, coconut milk and coconut yogurt in a blender until smooth.
2) Add ice and blend until there are no more ice chunks.
3) Serve immediately.

PHYTO GREEN

SERVES 1

You might be wondering why there are no recipes for green juices or smoothies in this book. It's for good reason. I'm a huge fan of the highly concentrated nutrition in marine phytoplankton (which I discuss in more detail in the How to Use this Book section, on page 31). My philosophy on this subject is to get your nutrition in the most concentrated and efficient form possible, and in my opinion, nothing beats phytoplankton. You'd be hard pressed (literally!) to find a green juice that contains as many nutrients as you can get in this drink, and it's so much easier to make, with barely any cleanup! I don't mix this into any smoothies because, quite frankly, why ruin a great smoothie! Get your boost of nutrition in from this drink, then enjoy your smoothie!

In Tulum, we elected to use pineapple as a base for this particular drink as it's abundant, and the flavor complements the phytoplankton really well; however, it also works with orange juice, and some people even prefer this. It's good to drink this quickly before the phytoplankton begins to oxidize (you'll notice that it will separate if sitting too long, and start to appear more brownish-green).

If you are nervous about the strong taste of the phytoplankton, start with $\frac{1}{4}$ or even $\frac{1}{8}$ teaspoon. It does have a strong taste (I think it tastes way better than spirulina, but as it comes from the ocean, it does have a bit of a sushi/seaweed flavor) although the way this drink is served, it's rare to find someone who really doesn't like it. I started my children off with barely anything and gradually built it up so that they didn't even notice. One day Kai came to me and said, "Mummy, I used to think that this phytoplankton thing was disgusting, but now I quite look forward to it"—I think his body recognised it was getting some good stuff!

INGREDIENTS:

¼ cup / 60g pineapple or orange juice

1½ tablespoons / 22g lime juice (optional)

½ - 1 cup / 64-128g water, or to taste

½ teaspoon / 2g marine phytoplankton powder

METHOD:

1) Mix the pineapple and lime juice with water.

2) Carefully add the phytoplankton powder and whisk until the powder is fully incorporated. Give it a stir if the phytoplankton starts to settle.

DANIELLA'S DAILY DOSE

SERVES 1

This drink affectionately got its name in the restaurant because it's what I ask for every day, and everyone else started following my lead! This is a step up in intensity from the Phyto Green (page 197), and contains a double dose of phytoplankton (one whole teaspoon). If you'd like to up it further, you certainly can; just add a little at a time, working your way up to a higher strength. I like to include marine collagen powder, making this one of the most nutritious liquid meals on the planet!

Keep this drink short and down it in a couple of gulps. It has a strong flavor from the phytoplankton, but the acidity of the lime adds nice balance. Personally, I omit the orange, but that's down to preference; I like it really sour!

INGREDIENTS:

⅓ cup / 42g orange juice
1½ tablespoons / 22g lime juice
½ -1 cup / 64-128g filtered water
1 teaspoon / 4g marine phytoplankton
1-2 tablespoons / 2-4g marine collagen powder

METHOD:

1) Whisk all ingredients together until phytoplankton and collagen are completely dissolved.

CHARCOAL LEMONADE

SERVES 1

Did you know that activated charcoal is used in hospitals for certain cases of poisoning and overdoses, as it has an incredible ability to absorb toxins? We have it on our drinks menu as a long drink, but also suggest this whenever someone has a delicate stomach. I've heard that it's great for hangovers, too!

If you live in a progressive part of the world, you are likely already familiar with charcoal drinks; if not, don't worry, the charcoal powder itself is tasteless but the drink looks impressive! Activated charcoal comes from a few sources including coconut shells–and of course, that's the one we use and recommend!

INGREDIENTS:

2 tablespoons / 28g lime juice

1½ tablespoons / 20g activated charcoal powder (from coconut shells)

2 teaspoons / 16g honey or maple syrup

1 cup / 128g mineral water

METHOD:

1) Stir all ingredients together and serve chilled or with ice.

CITRUS ELECTROLYTE

SERVES 1

This refreshing, electrolyte-boosting drink is just the thing to replace lost minerals in hot weather. It also does wonders after a workout, or if you have been under the weather. I love the mix of salt and sweet orange juice with just a touch of maple syrup. If you don't drink alcohol, you can almost fool yourself into thinking you are drinking a margarita!

INGREDIENTS:

pinch Himalayan pink salt + extra for the salt rim

¼ cup / 32g orange juice

1½ tablespoon / 22g lime juice

½ cup / 64g coconut water

2 teaspoons / 16g maple syrup

1 cup / 128g mineral water

METHOD:

1) Wet the rim of a glass; dip it into a shallow plate of salt to make a salt rim.
2) Whisk together all the ingredients, fill the prepared glass with ice, and pour over the drink.

MINDFUL MOJITO

SERVES 1

I don't drink alcohol, but every once in a while, I want a drink that feels like a cocktail. This alcohol-free twist on a traditional mojito hits all the same fresh, minty notes, but doesn't leave you fuzzy-headed! Don't skip the rosemary syrup—it's worth the effort as it provides such a wonderful depth of flavor.

FOR THE ROSEMARY SYRUP:

2 cups / 255g water

7 ounces / 200g fresh rosemary

1 cup / 250g muscovado sugar

FOR THE COCKTAIL:

1½ tablespoons / 22g rosemary syrup

½ lime, cut into small wedges

1 sprig of rosemary + extra for garnish

1 sprig of mint + extra for garnish

1½ tablespoons / 22g lime juice 1 cup / 128g mineral water

TO MAKE THE ROSEMARY SYRUP:

1) Combine the water and rosemary in a small saucepan and bring to a boil. Cook for 15 minutes, then strain and discard the rosemary.

2) Return the rosemary-infused water to the pan, add the muscovado sugar, and bring to a boil; simmer for 10 minutes.

3) Cool and store in an airtight container in the fridge for up to 2 weeks.

TO MAKE THE COKTAIL:

1) Muddle the rosemary syrup, lime wedges, rosemary and mint in a cocktail shaker.

2) Add the lime juice and mineral water and mix well.

3) Pour over ice and garnish with extra mint and fresh rosemary.

TURMERIC GINGER LATTE

SERVES 1

This is a top favorite in Tulum, where it's made with fresh turmeric & ginger juice. If you don't have these on hand, then turmeric and ginger powder also work well.

INGREDIENTS:
2 tablespoons / 28g ginger juice or ¼ teaspoon ginger powder

2 tablespoons / 28g turmeric juice or ¼ teaspoon turmeric powder

½ cup / 115g Coconut Milk (p. 215) or canned

pinch of black pepper

pinch of Himalayan pink salt

honey or maple syrup, to taste

METHOD:
1) If using powdered ginger and turmeric, start by mixing these into a paste with a small amount of coconut milk.
2) Combine the ginger and turmeric in a small saucepan with the coconut milk, black pepper, and salt; heat over low flame until almost simmering, then transfer to a mug.
3) Sweeten to taste with honey or maple syrup.

BUYAH CAFE/FUN GUY

SERVES 1

You may not believe me if I tell you the secret of where the name for this coffee came from! After writing menus for days, I was struggling to come up with names for recipes, so my dear friend Rhiannon (who was our on-staff nutritionist at the time) and I started getting silly with titles. Both being English, Rhiannon and I share the same Brit humor, and as a joke, I referred to one of Sasha Baron Cohen's aliases, Ali G, who was known for saying, "Booyah Kasha" to reference something great or well done (I'm not even sure how it would be written!). Somehow this name stuck, I changed the spelling, and now hear people all over the restaurant ordering their Buyah Cafe, probably imagining that this is some mysterious Mayan name for a blended coffee! Huge apologies if I've burst your bubble, but at the time, we just thought it was quite funny!

In this recipe, we replace butter or ghee from the typical butter coffee with coconut oil and cream (it also works well with a full fat coconut milk). The fat from the oil, and the coconut cream/milk, helps to balance out the caffeine for a more stable energy boost. I don't drink coffee anymore, but when I did, this was the only way I could enjoy it without getting the jitters.

Add your favorite medicinal mushroom blend to the mix (we use a blend of reishi, lion's mane, chaga and cordyceps) and 1½ tablespoons cacao powder to turn this into what we like to call a "Fun Guy Cafe" (sorry, playing on words became a bit of a theme when these recipes were birthed!).

INGREDIENTS:

1 shot / 56g espresso or ¼ cup coffee

1 tablespoon / 14g coconut oil

¾ cup / 160g Coconut Milk (p. 215), warmed

METHOD:

1) Blitz all ingredients in a blender and enjoy hot or over ice.

RICH HOT CHOCOLATE

SERVES 1

This rich, chocolatey drink, blended with a little coconut oil for extra-creamy texture, is perfect for rainy days. Hot chocolate is all about the quality of the cacao; I especially love the roasted Mexican cacao we use at the restaurant, but any good-quality cacao powder will work well.

Serve with Coconut Whipped Cream (page 238) and a good grating of dark chocolate on top for an even more decadent indulgence.

INGREDIENTS:

1½ teaspoons / 4g cacao powder
2 teaspoons / 10g coconut sugar
2 teaspoons / 14g maple syrup
1 tablespoon / 14g coconut oil
7 ounces / 200g Coconut Milk (p. 215) or canned
½ / 3g of a vanilla bean

METHOD:

1) Heat all ingredients in a small pot.
2) Pour into a blender and blend until well incorporated.
3) Serve hot (or if you prefer a cold drink, simply skip step 1, and pour over ice after blending).

CARDOMOM & GINGER CHAI

SERVES 4

I've been making fresh chai tea daily for almost ten years now, and after tweaking the recipe little by little over time, I've finally found my favorite version! Everyone knows that when they come over to our home in Los Angeles, there will be a pot of chai on the stove, and when I'm in Tulum, the team here makes me my special version!

I'm not a big fan of cinnamon in chai as it tends to dominate all the flavors (though it took me a long time to realize this!), so this recipe focuses on my favorite spice, cardamom, as the lead flavor, with a good boost of ginger, too. If you can make time to prepare fresh ginger juice, it really makes all the difference. Either run it through a standard juicer, or blend cut pieces with a small amount of water (just enough to get it to blend), and strain or gently squeeze through a nut milk bag (be careful, as ginger can irritate sensitive skin). Make a big batch and freeze in ice cube trays; once frozen, transfer them to a tub and pull out one or two whenever you make the chai. By the time the spices have boiled, the ginger should be thawed into liquid, especially if you keep it in a bowl near the boiling pot. You can keep boiling this pot down (it will simply concentrate more), adding more water and even keep to heat up again for the next days if you still have a lot left.

INGREDIENTS:

1 teaspoon / 3g cardamom seed, cracked
3 whole cloves
¼ piece star anise
pinch black pepper
1 cube frozen fresh ginger juice or 1" piece ginger, sliced
6 quart water
1 bag black tea

METHOD:

1) In a large pot, combine the cardamom, cloves, star anise, pepper, ginger (if using root), and water. Bring the mixture to a boil and simmer for 10-15 minutes.
2) Add the black tea and continue boiling for another 10 minutes, or until the tea strength is to your liking. Remove the tea bag.
3) Strain into mugs, and add a splash of ginger juice, plus coconut or almond milk and sugar to taste.
4) Sprinkle with extra black pepper, for a spicier flavor.

SUPER BLENDED BROTH

SERVES 1 `E`

This blended broth really is a superstar! Enjoy it as a regular nutrient infusion, or use it to boost you up if you are feeling low. There are many options when it comes to medicinal mushroom mixes, but I particularly like the benefits of reishi and lion's mane for their respective calming and immune-boosting properties. Once it's blended, sip on this creamy broth and feel the goodness being absorbed into your cells!

INGREDIENTS:

2 cups / 255g Chicken Bone Broth (p. 237)
¼" slice / 5g of ginger root
½" piece / 3g of turmeric root
1 tablespoon / 14g coconut oil
1 tablespoon / 15g collagen powder
½ teaspoon / 1g reishi & lion's mane powder (we use Om brand)
pinch Himalayan pink salt
pinch black pepper
1 lime wedge, to serve

METHOD:

1) Heat the bone broth in a saucepan. Transfer to a blender and add the remaining ingredients (except the lime).

2) Blend for 30 seconds to 1 minute—starting on the lowest speed and slowly increasing to the highest speed—or until the ginger root and turmeric root have been blended thoroughly.

3) Pour into a large mug and serve with a wedge of lime.

THE BASICS

At the restaurant, anything that can be made from scratch—almond and coconut milk, mayos and ketchup, broths, salsas—is, and I work hard to bring this same philosophy into my home kitchen. In a pinch, I'll sometimes turn to store-bought sauces or condiments (and most recipes in this book will work with good-quality packaged options), but because they're so often full of unwanted preservatives and sugar, they can really throw off an otherwise clean eating routine. Plus, when you take the time to make recipes from whole ingredients, everything tastes so much fresher and more flavorful! Some of these basics are super simple and can be thrown together quickly, while others may take a little longer to make. The important thing to remember is that none of them are difficult or require special equipment, and most can be doubled or tripled and stored in either the fridge or freezer for future use. Most also feature in multiple recipes throughout the book, so if you take the time to stock your fridge with, say, a batch of Coconut Cheese (p. 219), a few pizza bases (page 229), and a couple of sauces, you'll be able to throw together the Barbecue Pizza (page 141), Basil & Tomato Pizza (page 138), Quesadillas (page 121) and more, quickly and easily; not to mention giving you the tools to experiment with your own grain- and dairy-free creations!

COCONUT MILK

MAKES APPROXIMATELY 1.5 PINTS

There's really nothing like cracking open a fresh coconut and making milk from the slightly sweet flesh (if you need a tutorial, check out my guide to opening coconuts on page 37). This creamy coconut milk gets blended into our smoothies, whipped into dairy-free whipping cream, and provides the base for our famous Coconut Cheese (page 219). You can now find frozen coconut meat in many supermarkets, but if you're planning to cook with the milk (to make our coconut cheese, for example) be sure to buy only mature coconut meat, as the young meat won't provide the correct flavor or texture.

If, for whatever reason, you don't see yourself making this from scratch, canned coconut milk also works as a substitution in all of our recipes. Just opt for a brand that contains only coconut and water, with no added gums or sugar, if possible.

INGREDIENTS:

11oz / 300g fresh or frozen coconut meat (approximately one coconut), chopped into small pieces

2½ cups / 600 ml filtered water

METHOD:

1) Blend the coconut meat and water in a high-powered blender for 2-3 minutes.
2) Line a large pitcher with a nut milk bag and pour in the coconut milk. Gently squeeze the bag to extract all of the liquid.
3) Use immediately or store in an airtight bottle in the fridge for up to 4 days.

TIP: If you are making coconut milk with frozen coconut meat, don't worry about defrosting it; just use hot water in the mix.

ALMOND MILK

MAKES 1 QUART   **E**

Once you realize how easy it is to make almond milk (and how delicious it tastes), you will wonder why you ever bothered with the cartoned version. Plus, there's no wasteful packaging here!

If you have time, it's best to soak the almonds (or any other nuts/seeds you may choose to make into nut milk) overnight, or for a few hours at least. This helps to break down phytic acid, a protective substance that coats seeds and nuts and can inhibit the absorption of beneficial minerals.

You will need what's known as a nut milk bag, or a fine mesh cloth, to get the best-quality milk with no particles; but in a pinch, a very fine mesh sieve also works.

INGREDIENTS:
1 full cup / 165g almonds, soaked in filtered water overnight and drained
6-7 cups / 1550-1750g filtered water

METHOD:
1) In a blender, purée the almonds and water on high speed for about 1 minute.
2) Line a large pitcher with a cloth nut milk bag and pour over the almond milk. Gently squeeze the bag to extract all of the liquid.
3) Use immediately or store in an airtight bottle in the fridge for up to 4 days.

COCONUT SOUR CREAM

MAKES TWO-THIRDS OF A CUP

This simple to make, dairy-free sour cream is incredibly versatile (also incredibly delicious!), which is why you'll find it in so many of our recipes. The thicker the coconut cream, the thicker the end result will be.

INGREDIENTS:

1 can coconut milk or ⅔ cup / 145g cream from homemade Coconut Milk (p. 215)

1 tablespoon / 14g lime juice

1 tablespoon / 14g apple cider vinegar

pinch Himalayan pink salt

METHOD:

1) Place the coconut milk in the fridge overnight (this will allow the creamy part of the coconut milk to rise to the top and form a thick layer).

2) The next day, carefully scoop this thick creamy layer into a bowl. Add the lime juice, apple cider vinegar, and salt; whisk to combine.

3) Use immediately or store in an airtight container in the fridge for 3-4 days.

COCONUT CHEESE

MAKES APPROXIMATELY 1½ CUPS

Back to where it all started, this is the cheese that forms the basis of so many of our dishes, including our famous Quesadillas (page 121). With coconut milk as the base, it's very different from the majority of vegan cheeses out there, which tend to use mainly nuts (usually cashews), making them heavy and often difficult to digest.

The trick to this cheese is in the stirring. You'll get the very best result if you whisk constantly, allowing the agar to completely dissolve in. You'll know it's ready when you lift the whisk from the mixture and a ribbon falls back into the pot, holding its shape for a few seconds before slowly disappearing back into the cheese. Keep the cheese uncovered while cooling, then cover and transfer to the fridge to chill overnight. You should be able to slice it with a warm knife.

Agar agar is a seaweed-based alternative to gelatin and allows the cheese to set. Different brands of agar may provide different results. In the Stocking Up: Dry Ingredients section on page 32, you'll find suggestions of brands we have tested and verified. For a firmer cheese, you can increase the level of agar agar by 4 or 5 grams.

INGREDIENTS:

13.5 oz / 398ml Coconut Milk (p. 215), or canned
2 tablespoons / 20g tapioca
2¼ teaspoons / 8g agar agar
½ teaspoon / 5g Himalayan pink salt
¼ teaspoon / 2g apple cider vinegar
1 tablespoon / 8g nutritional yeast

METHOD:

1) Pour the coconut milk into a saucepan and whisk in the tapioca, agar, salt and vinegar.
2) Gently heat the mixture, whisking constantly to ensure that all the ingredients are dissolved.
3) Once thje mixture is hot, sprinkle over the nutritional yeast flakes, and continue to whisk until the yeast has dissolved and the mixture starts to thicken (about 15 minutes).
4) Pour into a storage container and let cool to room temperature, uncovered.
5) Cover and store in an airtight container in the fridge for up to 2 weeks.

CHIPOTLE COCONUT CHEESE

MAKES APPROXIMATELY 1½ CUPS

This is a simple way to add some serious flavor to our base cheese. If you like your cheese a little spicy, just add a little more paste! We use this melted over many of our dishes, so it's smart to have a batch in the fridge at all times. For a little flavor variation, feel free to use this in place of the base cheese in dishes such as our Quesadillas (page 121).

INGREDIENTS:

1 recipe Coconut Cheese (p. 219)
2 teaspoons / 14g Chipotle Chile Paste (p. 235)
1 teaspoon / 2g paprika
⅛ teaspoon / 1g Himalayan pink salt

METHOD:

1) Heat the coconut cheese in a small saucepan over medium-low flame. Add the chipotle chile paste, paprika and salt; whisk well to combine.

2) Use immediately or transfer to a storage container and cool to room temp. Chipotle cheese can be kept in the fridge for up to 1 week.

NACHO COCONUT CHEESE

MAKES 1 CUP

So cheesy, you won't even miss the dairy! At the restaurant, we use this cheese sauce in our Nachos (page 109) and Cauliflower Nacho Cheese (page 148), but I also love it drizzled over simply cooked vegetables or spiralized zucchini.

INGREDIENTS:

1½ tablespoons / 15g tapioca flour
1 tablespoon / 7g nutritional yeast
½ teaspoon / 4g Himalayan pink salt
¼ teaspoon / 1g black pepper
1 tablespoon / 9g ground flax
½ teaspoon/ 1g paprika
¼ teaspoon / 1g onion powder
¼ teaspoon / 1g garlic powder
1 cup / 240g Coconut Milk (p. 215) or canned
½ teaspoon / 2g apple cider vinegar

METHOD:

1) Whisk together the tapioca, nutritional yeast, salt, pepper, flax, paprika, onion powder and garlic powder in a small saucepan. Add the coconut milk and apple cider vinegar; whisk until smooth.

2) Cook over a low flame, whisking constantly until the mixture thickens and small bubbles form around the edge (about 10-15 minutes).

3) Use immediately or store in the fridge for up to 1 week. To reheat, simply pour into a saucepan and stir over low heat until warmed through.

TOASTED HEMP

MAKES 1½ CUPS

So easy to make, toasting hemp improves its flavor, which can otherwise be a little bitter. You can sprinkle these on literally everything!

INGREDIENTS:

1½ cups hemp seed

METHOD:

1) Preheat the oven to 350°F.
2) Spread the hemp seeds onto a sheet pan lined with parchment paper or a silicone mat. Toast in oven for about 20-30 minutes, rotating once halfway through.
3) Eat immediately or store in an airtight container for a month or more.

HEMP TAHINI

MAKES 1 CUP

We use hemp tahini as a base for several recipes, including salads, falafel, and our Veggie Burger (page 147). This keeps really well in the fridge and is useful to have on hand.

INGREDIENTS:

1½ cups Toasted Hemp

METHOD:

1) Place the toasted hemp in a food processor and purée, scraping down the sides as needed, until a smooth paste forms (about 20-30 minutes).
2) Use immediately or store in an airtight container in the fridge for up to 2 weeks.

ALMOND BUTTER

MAKES 1 CUP

Homemade almond butter is so easy to make and is a much better value than store-bought options. All you need are some almonds, a food processor, and a bit of time! Once the almonds are ground into a flour, don't worry if you don't see anything change for a while; at one point, it will turn into a paste and then the butter. Keep the processor running until the butter is smooth and runny.

INGREDIENTS:

2 cups / 320g almonds

METHOD:

1) Purée the almonds in a food processor until a smooth butter forms (about 20-30 minutes), scraping down sides periodically; it will be very warm.
2) Store in an airtight container in the fridge for several weeks.

COCONUT BACON

MAKES 1 CUP

I know this is a bit of an oxymoron, but if you are craving something with a smoky, "bacon-y" flavor, this vegan version is a delicious alternative. Eat this on its own as a snack, or sprinkle over salads, pizzas or anything else you like! If you have the time to make your own coconut strips, you'll be able to get them a little bigger, which I find provides the best taste and texture (see page 37 for how to open a coconut).

INGREDIENTS:

3 teaspoons / 15g coconut aminos

2 tablespoons / 30g liquid smoke

2 tablespoons / 40g maple syrup

1 cup / 80g coconut strips or packaged unsweetened coconut flakes

METHOD:

1) Preheat oven to 250°F.
2) Mix together the coconut aminos, liquid smoke, and maple syrup in a small bowl. Toss the coconut strips in the liquid, making sure they are evenly coated, and let sit for 5 minutes.
3) Spread out evenly on a sheet pan lined with parchment or a silicone mat and bake in the oven for about 45 minutes.
4) Turn off the oven (leaving the door closed) and let the coconut sit inside and dehydrate for 4-5 hours, until crispy and dry. Use immediately or store in an airtight container at room temperature for up to 2 weeks.

TIP: To crisp up before serving, pop in the oven for 5-10 minutes or heat gently in a skillet.

TOASTED SEEDS

MAKES 2 CUPS

I can't get enough of these toasted seeds and love to eat them as a snack, or to sprinkle over salads, soups, dips and more! You can use just pumpkin or sunflower seeds, a mix of the two, or mix it up with your other favorites. I love it when they pop while cooking! You may substitute a sprinkle of salt for the coconut aminos if you want a simpler taste.

INGREDIENTS:

1 cup / 135g sunflower seeds

1 cup / 150g pumpkin seeds

coconut aminos, to taste (approximately 1-2 tablespoons)

METHOD:

1) Place the seeds in a skillet set over medium flame. Stir continuously, ensuring that the seeds are toasting evenly and not burning. If the seeds start to "pop," simply lower the heat and keep stirring.

2) Once the seeds are nicely browned and toasted, add a dash of coconut aminos to the pan and stir in evenly.

3) Turn off the heat, let the seeds cool, and enjoy immediately or keep in an airtight container for up to 2 weeks.

PLANTAIN CHIPS

MAKES 1 CUP

When you are looking for a change from tortilla chips, plantain chips make a great alternative. Delicious on their own as a salty snack, sprinkled with cayenne pepper, or loaded up with guacamole, these can also be broken up into smaller pieces to use as a crouton replacement in salads. For a lighter option, toss the plantains with a little avocado oil and salt, bake in a 300°F oven for 30-40 minutes, turn off the oven, and let the plantains dry out for about 2 hours.

INGREDIENTS:

avocado oil for frying
2 green plantains
Himalayan pink salt

METHOD:

1) In a deep sauté pan, heat 1-1½ inches of avocado oil to 350°F.
2) Peel the plantains and slice them using a mandolin on the thinnest setting. Shallow fry the plantains until golden brown and crispy.
3) Drain over a wire rack or paper towel–lined plate and season with salt to taste.

PIZZA BASE

MAKES TWO 8" ROUNDS M

This is one of the first grain-free recipes I ever created, long before the Real Coconut had even been conceived! Grain-free pizza bases are no easy feat, but this vegan one, made with a combination of puréed cauliflower, tapioca flour and coconut flour, is so good you won't even miss delivery! These freeze beautifully, so I highly recommend keeping a stash in your freezer for pizza emergencies.

INGREDIENTS:

2 cups / 100g cauliflower florets, roughly chopped

1 (¼ oz) / 7g packet active dry yeast

3½ tablespoons / 25g warm water

1½ teaspoons / 5g maple syrup

⅔ cup / 75g tapioca flour

½ cup / 50g coconut flour

1 teaspoon / 3g ground chia

¼ teaspoon / 3g Himalayan pink salt

¾ teaspoon / 3g baking soda

3 tablespoons / 42g extra virgin olive oil

½ teaspoon / 2g apple cider vinegar

METHOD:

1) Preheat the oven to 350°F.

2) Boil the cauliflower in a small pot of water until very tender, about 5-8 minutes; drain well and transfer to a blender or food processor. Blend into a smooth purée and set aside.

3) In a small bowl, stir together the yeast, warm water, and maple syrup. Cover and put in a warm place to allow the yeast to activate; it will become very foamy.

4) In the bowl of a stand mixer, combine the tapioca, coconut flour, chia, salt, and baking soda. Add the olive oil, vinegar and puréed cauliflower; mix on low with the paddle attachment until incorporated. Add the yeast mixture and continue mixing until a smooth dough forms (about 3-5 minutes).

5) Separate the dough into 2 balls. Using a rolling pin, roll each ball into an 8-inch round, about ¼- to ½-inch thick, dusting with extra tapioca to prevent sticking if needed.

6) Par-bake for 10-12 minutes.

VEGAN MAYO

MAKES 2 CUPS

Our egg-free mayo is quick and easy to whip up, features in several recipes, and can be used as a dip, a dressing for salads, or whatever else you fancy!

INGREDIENTS:

2 cups / 400g Coconut Yogurt (p. 49) or store-bought
4 teaspoons / 40g Dijon mustard
zest of one lime
3 tablespoons / 50g extra virgin olive oil
¼ teaspoon / 3g Himalayan pink salt
¼ teaspoon / 2g black pepper
pinch ground turmeric

METHOD:

1) Place all ingredients in a blender and purée on medium speed for 1 minute.
2) Use immediately or store in an airtight container in the fridge for up to 1 week.

BAJA MAYO

MAKES 3/4 CUP   E

I can't get enough of this mayo! We serve it on the Baja Tacos (page 127) at the restaurant, but I also love dipping Baked Sweet Potato Fries (page 114) into it or spreading it on just about anything!

INGREDIENTS:

1 large egg
1 tablespoon / 14g lime juice
½ teaspoon / 2g Dijon mustard
1 teaspoon / 5g Chipotle Chile Paste (p. 235)
½ teaspoon / 4g Himalayan pink salt
pinch paprika
½ cup / 100g avocado oil

METHOD:

1) Bring a small pot of water to a boil. Gently lower in the egg and boil for 6 minutes; remove from the water and peel.
2) Place the egg, lime juice, Dijon mustard, chipotle chile paste, salt and paprika in a blender and purée until smooth. With the blender running, slowly drizzle in the avocado oil.
3) Use immediately or store in an airtight container in the fridge for up to 5 days.

TO MAKE A VEGAN VERSION:

¾ cup / 150g Coconut Yogurt (p. 49) or store-bought
1¼ teaspoons / 6g lime juice
3 teaspoons / 16g Dijon mustard
2 teaspoons / 10g chipotle paste
¼ teaspoon / 4g Himalayan pink salt
1 teaspoon / 2g paprika
3 tablespoons / 40g avocado oil

METHOD:

1) In a blender, combine the yogurt, lime juice, mustard, chipotle paste, salt and paprika.
2) With the blender running on medium speed, drizzle in avocado oil, and continue to blend for 1 minute.
3) Store in an airtight container in the fridge for up to 1 week.

CHIPOTLE CHILE PASTE

MAKES 2 CUPS

Chipotle—otherwise known as smoked jalapeño—is a base flavor of many of our dishes, and this chipotle paste is a must for re-creating the authentic flavors from the restaurant. Try freezing this in an ice cube tray so you've got easy access to small amounts, as needed.

INGREDIENTS:

1 tablespoon / 14g avocado oil
½ small / 50g onion, roughly chopped
4 / 1g bay leaves
1 teaspoon / 1g dried oregano
5 cloves / 25g garlic, roughly chopped
3 ounces / 75g dried chipotle chiles
1 medium / 60 Roma tomatoes, roughly chopped
16 ounce / 500ml filtered water
pinch Himalayan pink salt
pinch black pepper

METHOD:

1) Heat the avocado oil in a saucepan over medium heat. Add the onion, bay leaf, oregano and garlic and sauté until the onion is translucent. Add the chipotle chiles and tomatoes and sauté for 5 more minutes. Add water, salt and pepper; cover and simmer for at least 25 minutes.
2) Strain the mixture, being sure to reserve the liquid. Transfer to a blender and blitz until a paste forms, adding some of the reserved liquid as needed.
3) Use immediately or store in an airtight container in the fridge for up to 2 weeks or in the freezer for several months.

VEGETABLE STOCK

MAKES 2 QUARTS   M

Making vegetable stock is a perfect way to use up any leftover vegetables that are no longer fresh enough to enjoy on their own, which can really help to reduce food waste in a home kitchen. This base of carrots, celery and onion gives a great flavor, but no vegetable should be left behind (broccoli/cauliflower stems, mushrooms, squash—all veggie scraps are welcome)!

Having stock in the freezer makes life so much easier. You can freeze the stock in bigger containers for soups, or in ice cube trays to add a little flavor to vegetable dishes or sauces. Also feel free to treat this stock as a broth drink in its own right and season accordingly . . . coconut aminos, grain-free miso pastes, seaweeds and more can all go in!

INGREDIENTS:

10 medium carrots, roughly chopped
2 bunches celery, roughly chopped
3 medium onions, roughly chopped
5 / 2g bay leaves
3-5 sprigs fresh thyme
1 bunch parsley stems
1 bunch cilantro stems
1 teaspoon / 4g whole black peppercorns
2 cloves / 8g garlic
2 tablespoons / tomato paste

METHOD:

1) Place all ingredients in an 8-quart stock pot and cover with water, leaving about 2 inches at the top. Bring the mixture to a boil, then reduce the flame to a low simmer. Simmer gently for 4-6 hours.
2) Strain out the vegetables and pour the stock into airtight containers. Use immediately or store in the fridge for up to 1 week or in the freezer for several months.

CHICKEN BONE BROTH

MAKES 2 QUARTS

Bone broth has been around since the invention of cooking, but the Western world has only recently circled back and re-embraced its incredible health benefits. Making bone broth (or stock as our parents and grandparents called it) was a part of the ritual after enjoying a roast meal, and helped ensure that every element of the animal was respected and used. Making your own bone broth is not only far more economical than buying pre-made options, but also allows you to be clear about sourcing and what ingredients you choose to include. You can make this broth from the leftover bones after roasting a whole chicken, or purchase bones from a local, organic butcher. Once you have made the broth, I suggest storing it in smaller containers, and even filling one ice cube tray (or smaller pots) to have available for sauces.

INGREDIENTS:

- 3 pounds / 1.3kg bones from organic, pasture-raised chicken (necks, backs and feet are best)
- 6 medium carrots, roughly chopped
- 1 bunch celery, roughly chopped
- 2 medium onions, roughly chopped
- 5 / 2g bay leaves
- 3-5 sprigs fresh thyme
- 3-5 sprigs rosemary
- 1 bunch parsley stems
- 1 bunch cilantro stems
- 1 teaspoon / 4g whole black peppercorns
- 2 cloves / 8g garlic
- 2 tablespoons / 28g apple cider vinegar
- 4 quarts / 3.2kg water

METHOD:

1) Place all ingredients in an 8-quart stockpot and fill with water, leaving about an inch at the top. Bring the mixture to a boil, then reduce the heat to a low simmer. Allow to simmer for 6-8 hours (or overnight for a super rich broth), skimming the foam that accumulates at the surface as it cooks.

2) Strain and cool the broth. Use immediately or store in the fridge for up to a week or in the freezer for several months.

TIP: If you have a pressure cooker or Instant Pot, you can speed up the cooking time to only a couple of hours or less, and still extract all the goodness. See your appliance's instructions for further information.

RASPBERRY COULIS

MAKES 1 PINT

Coulis sounds fancy, but is actually super simple to make. I love it stirred into Coconut Yogurt (page 49), drizzled on pancakes, or spooned over pretty much any dessert.

INGREDIENTS:

2½ cups / 200g frozen raspberries
1 tablespoon / 15g coconut sugar
pinch Himalayan pink salt
1 tablespoon / 15g lime juice

METHOD:

1) Cook raspberries, coconut sugar and salt in a saucepan over low heat until the sugar dissolves and the raspberries are soft.
2) Transfer the mixture to a blender, add lime juice, and blend until smooth.
3) Strain through a sieve, and chill before using.

COCONUT WHIPPED CREAM

MAKES 1 CUP

A quick and easy dairy-free alternative to whipped cream, this goes well with most of our sweet treats, and even on our Rich Hot Chocolate (page 208). If you're using canned coconut milk, be sure to buy a brand that is free of any gums, as these sometimes keep the milk from separating properly.

INGREDIENTS:

1 can / 398ml Coconut Milk (p. 215)
1 tablespoon / 20g maple syrup

METHOD:

1) Place the coconut milk in the fridge overnight (this will allow the creamy part of the coconut milk to rise to the top and form a thick layer).
2) The next day, carefully scoop this thick creamy layer into a bowl. Add maple syrup and whisk until smooth, being careful not to over whip.

ACKNOWLEDGMENTS

The story of the Real Coconut—the restaurant, the brand, the recipes and this book—would not exist without the support of a whole host of people, and a somewhat unbelievable chain of events that has brought us to where we are now. This is my moment to say thank you, to all those who have been part of this story . . .

My father, who sometimes made me laugh so hard that I ended up in the emergency room with an asthma attack, and was the first person who taught me to question the "norms" and to look for better ways of doing things. My mother, who sat up with me for so many nights when I was a child, and taught me about kindness and generosity at a deep level through her art, and who I can always count on for heartfelt advice, even when things are not so easy.

My children, Luca and Kai, who, while so different, have both supported me on this journey, as it took us from the UK, to Mexico, and now to Los Angeles; both tolerant and understanding of my mission, and the time that I dedicate to it.

My Charlie, my husband and true essential support. I would not be who I am now, or doing all I do, without his belief and support in championing my vision.

And of course, nothing would happen without our Real Coconut teams . . .

In Tulum, the Real Coconut restaurant teams, past and current, who have been delivering life-changing food on a daily basis for five years! A special call-out to Clementine Didi, our Restaurant Manager, and Head Chef Janeth Vela, my dream team who make it all happen. Not forgetting also our Sanará Tulum hotel teams, who weave into the tapestry of the restaurant, supporting behind the scenes.

In Los Angeles, our dear Yan Quan, who has been my right-hand support for several years now. From developing recipes and future products to overseeing production runs and navigating production challenges, Yan handles so much, and has been the key to ensuring that the quality of food and products meet my (very strict!) standards.

In Minneapolis, Mike McKeon, who has been on our products team from day one, and who oversees all that relates to our products. And our growing products team, who stay bundled up in the cold weather, working hard and keeping a sense of humor, even though they are so far from the beaches of Tulum, and Los Angeles!

My dear brother Mark, who launched our products into the UK market, and who truly believes in, and stands by, our vision. I'm so grateful that we are able to work alongside each other.

Other friends and colleagues whom I cannot omit: Valeria, Richard, Juliana & Erik, John Kendall, Rhiannon Baker, Amanda Ferrario, Lauriane Gerard, Josh Jackson, Sarah Hall, Mike Schall, Betsy Foster, Nigel Miguel, Erica Volltrauer, Bernie Cahill, Jaime Murray, Dave Koorndyk, the Robles family, Anthony Esquivel, Lia Ronnen, and our cookbook production team: Thea Baumann, Anna Fishkin, Marie Reginato and Laney Clark.

This certainly is a long list to acknowledge, but that's really the point . . . this story isn't just my own. As Shakespeare said, "All the world's a stage, and all the men and women, merely players." This particular play has a lot of parts! Thank you to all those who have been part of, who are part of, and those who will play into the future of this story. My heart is filled with gratitude and love for you all.

INDEX

agar agar powder, 32
Al Pastor Tacos, 125
almonds. See nuts and seeds
apples
    about: organic vs non-organic, 27
    Apple & Cinnamon Cereal, 50–51
    Apple Cider Donuts, 155
    Stewed Apple & Dulce de Leche Quesadilla, 175
arrowroot starch, 32
asparagus, in Eggs Benedict, 76
avocados
    Avo, Radish & Jalapeño Salad, 88–89
    Avocado Gazpacho, 101
    Avocado Toast, 65
    Baja Tacos, 127
    Breakfast Tacos, 71
    Broccoli, Pea & Avocado Salad, 98
    Chilaquiles, 75
    Jalapeño & Radish Guacamole, 80
    Tinga Tacos, 128–29

bacon, coconut, 225
Bagels, 67
Baja Mayo, 232
Baja Tacos, 127
Baked Sweet Potato Fries, 114–15
bananas. See also plantains
    Banana Bread, 157
    Banana Split, 189
    Choco Nutty, 186–87
    Mint Choc, 188
    Strawberries & Cream, 190–91
Barbecue Pizza, 141
Barbecue Tostada, 113
base ingredients, 28–29
basic recipes, 213–37
    about: overview of, 41, 213
    Almond Butter, 223
    Almond Milk, 216
    Baja Mayo, 232
    BBQ Sauce, 234
    Chicken Bone Broth, 237
    Chipotle Chile Paste, 235
    Chipotle Coconut Cheese, 220
    Coconut Bacon, 225
    Coconut Cheese, 219
    Coconut Flour Tortilla Chips, 45
    Coconut Flour Tortillas, 43
    Coconut Milk, 215
    Coconut Sour Cream, 217
    Coconut Whipped Cream, 238
    Hemp Tahini, 222
    Ketchup, 233
    Nacho Coconut Cheese, 221
    Pizza Base, 229
    Plantain Chips, 227
    Raspberry Coulis, 238
    Toasted Hemp, 222
    Toasted Seeds, 226
    Vegan Mayo, 230–31
    Vegetable Stock, 236
Basil & Tomato Pizza, 138
BBQ Sauce, 234
berries
    about: organic vs non-organic, 27
    Blueberry Chia Jam, 62–63
    Blueberry Yogurt Popsicle, 171
    Raspberry Coulis, 238
    Seasonal Chia Parfait, 55
    Strawberries & Cream, 190–91
Blended Chocolate Chia Pudding, 53
blueberries. See berries
bone broth, chicken, 237
breads and pastries
    Apple Cider Donuts, 155
    Avocado Toast, 65
    Bagels, 67
    Banana Bread, 157
    Buttermilk Donuts, 156
    Cinnamon Rolls, 166–67
    Plantain Bread Croutons, 96–97
    Plantain Flour Bread, 60–61
    Raisin Scones, 164–65
    Toast & Spreads, 62–63
breakfast, 47–77
    about: overview of, 47
    Apple & Cinnamon Cereal, 50–51
    Avocado Toast, 65
    Bagels, 67
    Blended Chocolate Chia Pudding, 53
    Blueberry Chia Jam, 62–63
    Breakfast Tacos, 71
    Buttermilk Pancakes, 58–59
    Chilaquiles, 75
    Chocolate Cereal, 52
    Chocolate Hazelnut Spread, 62–63
    Coconut Yogurt, 49
    Eggs Benedict, 76–77
    Macho Pancakes, 57
    Plantain Flour Bread, 60–61
    Ranchero Eggs, 72–73
    Savory Jalapeño Waffles, 70
    Seasonal Chia Parfait, 55
    Sweet Potato & Plantain Hash Browns, 68–69
    Toast & Spreads, 62–63

broccoli
　Broccoli, Pea & Avocado Salad, 9
　Broccoli Soup, 102–3
broths and stock
　Chicken Bone Broth, 237
　Golden Broth, 105
　Super Blended Broth, 211
　Vegetable Stock, 236
Brownies, 169
bulk, preparing in, 35
burgers, veggie, 147
Burrito Bowl, 136–37
Buttermilk Donuts, 156
Buttermilk Pancakes, 58–59
Buyah Cafe/Fun Guy, 207

cabbage
　Baja Tacos, 127
　Creamy Slaw, 94
　Tinga Tacos, 128–29
cacao (chocolate)
　Banana Split, 189
　Blended Chocolate Chia Pudding, 53
　Brownies, 169
　Choco Nutty, 186–87
　Chocolate Cereal, 52
　Chocolate Chip Cookies, 159
　Chocolate Hazelnut Spread, 62–63
　Chocolate Mousse, 176–77
　Dulce de Leche Truffles, 172–73
　Macho Cacao Cake, 180–81
　Mint Choc, 188
　Rich Hot Chocolate, 208–9
Cardamom & Ginger Chai, 210
carrots, in Vegetable Stock, 236
cassava (yucca)
　about: flour, 32; stocking up, 33; virtues and uses, 31
　Fish & Chips, 131
　Yucca Croquettes, 110–11
　Yucca Fries, 116
cauliflower
　Burrito Bowl, 136–37
　Cauliflower Nacho Cheese, 148–49
　Cauliflower Rice, 136–37
　Pizza Base, 229 (See also pizza)
　Roasted Cauliflower Soup, 104
ceviche, coconut, 122–23
chai, cardamom and ginger, 210
Charcoal Lemonade, 200–201
Charred Sweet Potato Salad, 99
cheese
　about: non-dairy alternatives, 11, 28–29
　Basil & Tomato Pizza, 138
　Cauliflower Nacho Cheese, 148–49
　Chilaquiles, 75
　Chipotle Coconut Cheese, 220
　Coconut Cheese, 219
　Green Tomatillo Enchiladas, 142–43
　Loaded Sweet Potato Skins, 151

　Mushroom & Tomato Enchiladas, 145
　Nacho Bowl, 135
　Nacho Coconut Cheese, 221
　Nachos, 109
　Nutty Parmesan, 96–97
　Quesadillas, 121
　Spinach Cheese Dip, 87
　Spinach Cheese Pizza, 139
　Yucca Croquettes, 110–11
chicken
　Barbecue Pizza, 141
　Barbecue Tostada, 113
　Burrito Bowl, 136–37
　Chicken Bone Broth, 237
　Crumbed Chicken Bites, 132–33
　Golden Broth, 105
　Green Tomatillo Enchiladas, 142–43
　Nacho Bowl, 135
　Sopa de Lima (Lime Soup), 107
　Super Blended Broth, 211
　Tinga Tacos, 128–29
Chilaquiles, 75
Chipotle Chile Paste, 235
Chipotle Coconut Cheese, 220
chips, coconut flour tortilla, 45
chips, plantain, 227
Choco Nutty, 186–87
chocolate. See cacao (chocolate)
Chutney, 117
Cinnamon Rolls, 166–67
citrus
　Charcoal Lemonade, 200–201
　Citrus Electrolyte, 200–201
　Daniella's Daily Dose, 198–99
　Sopa de Lima (Lime Soup), 107
Cococcino, 193
coconut(s)
　about: aminos, 32; flour, 32; making milk, 37; milk, 32, 183; opening, 37; products from and to stock, 30, 32; selecting, 37; virtues and uses, 30
　Chipotle Coconut Cheese, 220
　Coconut Bacon, 225
　Coconut Ceviche, 122–23
　Coconut Cheese, 219
　Coconut Flour Tortilla Chips, 45
　Coconut Flour Tortillas, 43
　Coconut Milk, 215
　Coconut Sour Cream, 217
　Coconut Whipped Cream, 238
　Coconut Yogurt, 49
　drinks/smoothies with (See drinks and smoothies)
　Nacho Coconut Cheese, 221
　Super Sprinkles, 49
coffee/espresso
　Buyah Cafe/Fun Guy, 207
　Cococcino, 193
coulis, raspberry, 238
Creamy Slaw, 94
croquettes, yucca, 110–11

Crumbed Chicken Bites, 132–33

dairy-free. See grain-, gluten-, and dairy-free
Daniella's Daily Dose, 198–99
dates, in Chocolate Cereal, 52
donuts, apple cider, 155
donuts, buttermilk, 156
drinks and smoothies, 183–211
    about: Coconut Milk for, 183; overview of, 183
    Banana Split, 189
    Buyah Cafe/Fun Guy, 207
    Cardamom & Ginger Chai, 210
    Charcoal Lemonade, 200–201
    Choco Nutty, 186–87
    Citrus Electrolyte, 200–201
    Cococcino, 193
    Daniella's Daily Dose, 198–99
    Mango Lassi, 194–95
    Melon Mint Cooler, 194–95
    Mindful Mojito, 203
    Mint Choc, 188
    Phyto Green, 197
    Rich Hot Chocolate, 208–9
    Strawberries & Cream, 190–91
    Super Blended Broth, 211
    Turmeric Ginger Latte, 205
    Vanilla Almond Bliss, 185
dry ingredients to stock, 32
dulce de leche
    Dulce de Leche Truffles, 172–73
    Stewed Apple & Dulce de Leche Quesadilla, 175

egg replacers, 29
eggs
    Breakfast Tacos, 71
    Eggs Benedict, 76–77
    Ranchero Eggs, 72–73
electrolyte-boosting drink, 200–201
enchiladas, green tomatillo, 142–43
enchiladas, mushroom and tomato, 145
equipment, 35

falafel, hemp, 117
fish
    Al Pastor Tacos, 125
    Baja Tacos, 127
    Coconut Ceviche, 122–23
    Eggs Benedict, 76–77
    Fish & Chips, 131
    Fish Tacos, 126
flour, types of, 32
fries, baked sweet potato, 114–15
fries, yucca, 116

gazpacho, avocado, 101
ginger
    Cardamom & Ginger Chai, 210
    Ginger Cake, 179
    Ginger Snap Cookies, 160–61
    Ginger Vinaigrette, 91
    Turmeric Ginger Latte, 205
Golden Broth, 105
grain-, gluten-, and dairy-free
    about: overview of, 25
    dairy alternatives, 25
    Daniella's background and, 10–11
    getting started, 21
    grain-free flour alternatives, 25
    hidden grain/gluten sources, 25
    plant-focused eating and, 23
    pseudo-grains and, 25
    Real Coconut menu and, 15–16
grapes
    about: organic vs non-organic, 27
    Melon Mint Cooler, 194–95
Green Caesar Salad, 96–97
Green Tomatillo Enchiladas, 142–43
guacamole, jalapeño and radish, 80

hash browns, sweet potato and plantain, 68–69
hemp
    about: nutritional benefits, 31; sustainability of, 31
    Apple & Cinnamon Cereal, 50–51
    Chocolate Cereal, 52
    Hemp Falafel, 117
    Hemp Raisin Cookies, 163
    Hemp Tahini, 222
    Hemp Tahini Dip, 84
    Super Sprinkles, 49
    Toasted Hemp, 222
    Veggie Burger, 147
hero ingredients, 30–31
Hollandaise Sauce, 76
hot drinks
    Buyah Cafe/Fun Guy, 207
    Cardamom & Ginger Chai, 210
    Rich Hot Chocolate, 208–9
    Super Blended Broth, 211
    Turmeric Ginger Latte, 205

ingredients to stock. See also specific main ingredients
    base ingredients, 28–29
    dry ingredients, 32
    fresh produce, 33
    hero ingredients, 30–31
    organic vs non-organic, 27
    quality importance, 27

jackfruit
    about: dehydrated, 32; as protein alternative, 23
    Al Pastor Tacos, 125
    Barbecue Pizza, 141
    Barbecue Tostada, 113
    Green Tomatillo Enchiladas, 142–43
    Nacho Bowl, 135
    Tinga Tacos, 128–29
jalapeños. *See peppers*

kale
- about: appeal of baby kale, 95
- Baby Kale Salad, 95
- Golden Broth, 105
- Super Green Salad, 91

Ketchup, 233
key to recipe symbols, 39
kitchen equipment, 35

lattes, 205, 207
legumes, 29
lemon. See citrus
light bites, 109–17. See also salads and dressings; soups
- about: overview of recipes, 79
- Baked Sweet Potato Fries, 114–15
- Barbecue Tostada, 113
- Hemp Falafel, 117
- Nachos, 109
- Yucca Croquettes, 110–11
- Yucca Fries, 116

lime. See citrus
Liquid Smoke, 32
Loaded Sweet Potato Skins, 151

Macho Cacao Cake, 180–81
Macho Pancakes, 57
Mango Lassi, 194–95
marine phytoplankton
- about: importance, virtues and uses of, 31, 197; taste of, 197
- Daniella's Daily Dose, 198–99
- Phyto Green, 197

Mayan Tzikil Pak Dip, 83
mayo, Baja, 232
mayo, vegan, 230–31
Melon Mint Cooler, 194–95
milk, nondairy
- about: Coconut Milk, 32, 37; opening coconuts for, 37
- Almond Milk, 216
- Coconut Milk, 215

Mindful Mojito, 203
mint, in Melon Mint Cooler, 194–95
Mint Choc, 188
mojito mocktail, 203
mousse, chocolate, 176–77
mushrooms
- about: as protein alternatives, 23
- Coconut Ceviche, 122–23
- Loaded Sweet Potato Skins, 151
- Mushroom & Tomato Enchiladas, 145
- Spinach Cheese Pizza, 139
- Super Blended Broth, 211

Nacho Bowl, 135
nacho cheese, cauliflower, 148–49
Nacho Coconut Cheese, 221
Nachos, 109
nuts and seeds. See also hemp
- about: cashews, 28–29; egg replacers, 29; grinding seeds, 29; ground/grinding chia and flax, 29; nuts, 28–29; peanuts, 28; as protein alternatives, 23
- Almond Butter, 223
- Almond Milk, 216
- Apple & Cinnamon Cereal, 50–51
- Blended Chocolate Chia Pudding, 53
- Blueberry Chia Jam, 62–63
- Choco Nutty, 186–87
- Chocolate Cereal, 52
- Chocolate Chip Cookies, 159
- Chocolate Hazelnut Spread, 62–63
- Ginger Snap Cookies, 160–61
- Hemp Raisin Cookies, 163
- Mayan Tzikil Pak Dip, 83
- Nutty Parmesan, 96–97
- Seasonal Chia Parfait, 55
- Super Sprinkles, 49
- Toasted Seeds, 226
- Vanilla Almond Bliss, 185
- Veggie Burger, 147

oils, 28
organic vs non-organic produce, 27

pancakes and waffles
- Buttermilk Pancakes, 58–59
- Macho Pancakes, 57
- Savory Jalapeño Waffles, 70

parfait, seasonal chia, 55
peas, in Broccoli, Pea & Avocado Salad, 98
peppers
- Avo, Radish & Jalapeño Salad, 88–89
- Chipotle Chile Paste, 235
- Jalapeño & Radish Guacamole, 80
- Savory Jalapeño Waffles, 70

Phyto Green, 197
phytoplankton. See marine phytoplankton
Pico de Gallo, 81
pineapple, 125, 141, 194, 197
pizza
- Barbecue Pizza, 141
- Basil & Tomato Pizza, 138
- Pizza Base, 229
- Spinach Cheese Pizza, 139

plantains
- about: 33; buying, 33; drying (dried plantain mix), 50; flour, 31, 32; ripeness levels and ripening, 33; virtues and uses, 30–31
- Apple & Cinnamon Cereal, 50–51
- Chocolate Cereal, 52
- Hemp Falafel, 117
- Macho Pancakes, 57
- Plantain Bread Croutons, 96–97
- Plantain Chips, 227
- Plantain Flour Bread, 60–61
- Sweet Potato & Plantain Hash Browns, 68–69
- Toast & Spreads, 62–63
- Veggie Burger, 147

plant-focused eating. *See also* grain-, gluten-, and dairy-free
    about, 23
    author's (Daniella's) background and, 10–11
    grain-, gluten-, dairy-free and (*See also grain, gluten, and dairy-free*)
    Mexico, Mexican food and, 11
    protein alternatives, 23
    Real Coconut origins and, 15–16
plates, 119–51. *See also* pizza
    about: overview of recipes, 119
    Al Pastor Tacos, 125
    Baja Tacos, 127
    Burrito Bowl, 136–37
    Cauliflower Nacho Cheese, 148–49
    Coconut Ceviche, 122–23
    Crumbed Chicken Bites, 132–33
    Fish & Chips, 131
    Fish Tacos (vegan option), 126
    Green Tomatillo Enchiladas, 142–43
    Loaded Sweet Potato Skins, 151
    Mushroom & Tomato Enchiladas, 145
    Nacho Bowl, 135
    Quesadillas, 121
    Tinga Tacos, 128–29
    Veggie Burger, 147
popsicles, blueberry yogurt, 171
probiotic capsules, 32
produce to stock, 33. *See also* specific fruits and vegetables
protein alternatives, 23
psyllium husk powder/flakes, 32

quesadilla, stewed apple and dulce de leche, 175
Quesadillas (savory), 121

radishes
    Avo, Radish & Jalapeño Salad, 88–89
    Jalapeño & Radish Guacamole, 80
    Radish & Arugula Salad, 93
raisins
    Hemp Raisin Cookies, 163
    Raisin Scones, 164–65
Ranchero Eggs, 72–73
Ranchero Sauce, 72
Real Coconut
    Daniella's background and, 10–11
    GMOs, food sensitivities and, 15
    Malibu location, 19
    menu development, 15–16, 21
    Mexico, Mexican food and, 11
    origins and evolution of, 11, 15–16
    philosophy/mission driving, 9, 15, 19
    Sanará hotel and, 15, 19
    sustainability and, 15, 19
    today, 19
    Tulum location, 15–16, 19

recipes. *See also* ingredients to stock; specific main ingredients
    equipment for preparing, 35
    as plant-focused, 23
    preparing in bulk, 35
    protein alternatives, 23
    symbols key, 39
Red Enchilada Sauce, 145
Rich Hot Chocolate, 208–9
Roasted Cauliflower Soup, 104

salads and dressings, 88–99. *See also* Nacho Bowl
    about: overview of recipes, 79
    Avo, Radish & Jalapeño Salad, 88–89
    Baby Kale Salad, 95
    Broccoli, Pea & Avocado Salad, 98
    Charred Sweet Potato Salad, 99
    Creamy Slaw, 94
    Ginger Vinaigrette, 91
    Green Caesar Salad (and Dressing), 96–97
    Plantain Bread Croutons, 96–97
    Radish & Arugula Salad, 93
    Super Green Salad, 91
    Vegan Ranch Dressing, 94
    Vinaigrette, 99
salt, using and types, 28
Sanará, 15, 19, 53, 159
sauces, dips, and spreads
    Baja Mayo, 232
    BBQ Sauce, 234
    Chipotle Chile Paste, 235
    Chutney, 117
    Ginger Vinaigrette, 91
    Green Caesar Dressing, 96–97
    Hemp Tahini Dip, 84
    Hollandaise Sauce, 76
    Jalapeño & Radish Guacamole, 80
    Ketchup, 233
    Marinades (for tacos), 125, 126
    Mayan Tzikil Pak Dip, 83
    Pico de Gallo, 81
    Ranchero Sauce, 72
    Red Enchilada Sauce, 145
    Spinach Cheese Dip, 87
    Tinga Sauce, 128–29
    Tomatillo Sauce, 142
    Tomato Sauce, 110–11
    Vegan Mayo, 230–31
    Vegan Ranch Dressing, 94
    Vinaigrette, 99
sauces and spreads, sweet
    Blueberry Chia Jam, 62–63
    Chocolate Hazelnut Spread, 62–63
    Raspberry Coulis, 238
Savory Jalapeño Waffles, 70
scones, raisin, 164–65
Seasonal Chia Parfait, 55

snacks/small plates. *See light bites*
Sopa de Lima (Lime Soup), 107
soups, 101–7
    Avocado Gazpacho, 101
    Broccoli Soup, 102–3
    Golden Broth, 105
    Roasted Cauliflower Soup, 104
    Sopa de Lima (Lime Soup), 107
sour cream, coconut, 217
spinach
    about: organic vs non-organic, 27
    Loaded Sweet Potato Skins, 151
    other salads with, 93, 96–97
    soups with, 101, 102–3
    Spinach Cheese Dip, 87
    Spinach Cheese Pizza, 139
    Super Green Salad, 91
    Veggie Burger, 147
sprouts
    egg dishes with, 72–73, 76–77
    other recipes with, 65, 122, 125, 135
    salads with, 91, 95, 96–97, 98, 99
Stewed Apple & Dulce de Leche Quesadilla, 175
stock, vegetable, 236
strawberries. *See berries*
sugar and other sweeteners, 28
Super Blended Broth, 211
Super Green Salad, 91
Super Sprinkles, 49
sustainability, 15, 19
sweet potatoes
    Baked Sweet Potato Fries, 114–15
    Breakfast Tacos, 71
    Charred Sweet Potato Salad, 99
    Golden Broth, 105
    Hemp Falafel, 117
    Loaded Sweet Potato Skins, 151
    Sweet Potato & Plantain Hash Browns, 68–69
    Veggie Burger, 147
sweet treats, 153–81
    about: overview of, 153
    Apple Cider Donuts, 155
    Banana Bread, 157
    Blueberry Yogurt Popsicle, 171
    Brownies, 169
    Buttermilk Donuts, 156
    Chocolate Chip Cookies, 159
    Chocolate Mousse, 176–77
    Cinnamon Rolls, 166–67
    Coconut Whipped Cream, 238
    Dulce de Leche Truffles, 172–73
    Ginger Cake, 179
    Ginger Snap Cookies, 160–61
    Hemp Raisin Cookies, 163
    Macho Cacao Cake, 180–81
    Raisin Scones, 164–65
    Raspberry Coulis, 238
    Stewed Apple & Dulce de Leche Quesadilla, 175

sweeteners, 28
symbols key, 39

tacos
    Al Pastor Tacos, 125
    Baja Tacos, 127
    Breakfast Tacos, 71
    Fish Tacos (vegan option), 126
    marinades for, 125, 126
tahini, hemp, 222
tahini dip, hemp, 84
tapioca flour, 32
Tinga Sauce, 128–29
Toasted Hemp, 222
Toasted Seeds, 226
Tomatillo Sauce, enchiladas and, 142
tomatoes
    about: organic vs non-organic, 27
    Ketchup, 233
    Mayan Tzikil Pak Dip, 83
    Mushroom & Tomato Enchiladas, 145
    pizza with (See pizza)
    sauces with (See sauces, dips, and spreads)
tortillas. *See also tacos*
    about: flour for, 32; recipe development, 11
    Barbecue Tostada, 113
    Chilaquiles, 75
    Coconut Flour Tortilla Chips, 45
    Coconut Flour Tortillas, 43
    Nacho Bowl, 135
    Nachos, 109
    Quesadillas, 121
    Stewed Apple & Dulce de Leche Quesadilla, 175
tostadas, barbecue, 113
truffles, dulce de leche, 172–73
Turmeric Ginger Latte, 205

Vanilla Almond Bliss, 185
Vegan Mayo, 230–31
Vegan Ranch Dressing, 94
Vegetable Stock, 236
Veggie Burger, 147
Vinaigrettes, 91, 99

waffles, savory jalapeño, 70
whipped cream, coconut, 238

xanthan gum, 32

yogurt
    Baja Mayo (vegan), 232
    Blueberry Yogurt Popsicle, 171
    Coconut Yogurt, 49
    Super Sprinkles, 49
    Vegan Mayo, 230–31
yucca. *See cassava*

Daniella Hunter is the founder of the Real Coconut restaurants and products, and boutique wellness hotel Sanará Tulum. She is constantly working to ensure that her restaurants, recipes and products encompass her philosophy for sustainable eating and living: to support ourselves, while also caring for the planet. She and her family split their time between Tulum and Los Angeles.

To find out more about Daniella and her brands, visit daniellahunter.com

To learn more about the Real Coconut restaurants and shop our Real Coconut Market, visit realcoconutkitchen.com